Easy
GLUTEN
FREE

To my parents, George and Sofia, thank you
for instilling in me a passion for beautiful food
made with generosity and love.

Easy GLUTEN FREE

100+ delicious gluten-free recipes
the whole family will love!

HELEN TZOUGANATOS

plum. Pan Macmillan Australia

INTRODUCTION

As a mum of three young kids I need an arsenal of fuss-free family recipes to get me through a busy week. Juggling work, household chores, school activities, sport and homework can be challenging, and my husband and I often only have 20 minutes to get a nourishing meal on the table to appease 'staaaaarving' children. If you can relate to this daily struggle then this book is for you. My goal is to arm you with delicious, nutrient-dense, gluten-free recipes that will become your go-to meals. Along the way I will also share my cooking shortcuts and gluten-free tips and tricks. My recipes are simple, flavoursome and wholesome, and do not involve complex preparation or ingredients lists – who has time for that?

In our family of five only my eldest daughter and I need to follow a gluten-free diet (I am a coeliac and she is gluten-intolerant). It makes no difference to the other family members that my spaghetti with pork and veal meatballs (page 140) or baked quinoa-crumbed chicken with lime aioli (page 170) are gluten free; to them it's just delicious food made from scratch.

Kids are only concerned about how food tastes, but as a parent I'm always trying to sneak more goodness onto their plates to nourish their growing bodies with healthy proteins, vitamins, minerals and antioxidants. Unfortunately, kids aren't eating enough veggies these days, but I find interesting techniques, such as sautéing brussels sprouts with crispy pancetta (page 114), to make them much more enticing.

For me, cooking has always been about love, generosity and abundance. I can thank my Greek heritage for that. Some of the meals in this book are traditional Greek recipes handed down to me by my mother, but I cook a broad variety of cuisines at home – particularly Italian, Mexican, Lebanese and Chinese – and you will find a sprinkling of these throughout the book. I always try to cook with organic seasonal fruit and vegetables and ethically sourced animal proteins to maximise nutrient content and flavour.

All my recipes are uncomplicated, from an express midweek meal to a slow Sunday braise. I have also included many one-pot and one-tray dishes that require minimal prep and clean up but deliver maximum flavour. I like to inject complexity into my dishes by using a combination of dried and fresh herbs and spices, such as za'atar, sumac and oregano, and other miracle ingredients like tahini, lemon and balsamic vinegar for an acidic punch.

My gluten-free journey started 12 years ago when I discovered I was a coeliac during IVF treatment. Back then there were not many gluten-free ingredients on offer; supermarkets were not selling quinoa and if I requested tamari or buckwheat flour I was generally met with a blank stare. Thankfully the gluten-free market has exploded as more people are eliminating gluten for medical reasons or as a health choice, so these pantry staples are now readily available in most supermarkets or online. If you have the basics and a few fresh ingredients it is easy to whip up myriad gluten-free meals.

Over the years I have exhibited at several gluten-free expos around Australia and I've observed the growing number of people who not only avoid gluten but other food categories such as dairy and egg, too. Almost half the people who bought my baking cookbook *Hungry and Fussy* told me they also avoid dairy. For this reason, more than half the recipes in this book are also dairy free or cater to vegetarian, vegan or low-carb diets. Look out for the following symbols:

DF = DAIRY FREE

GF = GLUTEN FREE

LC = LOW CARB

V = VEGETARIAN

VG = VEGAN

I follow the 80/20 rule when it comes to eating. I eat wholesome, nourishing meals during the week and tend to indulge and bake on the weekend to satisfy my chocolate cravings.

All the recipes in this book have been tested by the toughest critics: my three kids. There is nothing more heartbreaking than pouring time and energy into a meal only to have it rejected when it hits the table, so I can assure you there is nothing too weird and not 'kid approved' here. I have included all their favourites, such as Ruby's Asian glazed salmon (page 162), Sofia's healthy crumbed fish fingers (page 150) and Vasili's chicken avgolemono soup (page 80). There are also the dishes loved by all, such as sticky pork ribs with tamari, honey & mustard glaze (page 194) and our cover star, lamb shanks with a pomegranate–balsamic glaze sitting on a bed of nourishing quinoa (page 222). I still recall the kids fighting over the last lamb shank when I was recipe writing, and immediately knew this had to be the cover dish.

This book is not just for people following a gluten-free diet. It is for anyone wanting uncomplicated, nourishing recipes to prepare and eat with the people they love. Please fill the pages with scribbles, notes and variations and make each recipe your own. I don't want this to be a coffee table cookbook; it is a practical family cookbook that I hope you will return to again and again for inspiration. I truly hope it instils you with the confidence to expand your cooking repertoire and delight your family with scrumptious gluten-free meals they will devour with pleasure.

Helen

11 COMMON MISTAKES HOME COOKS MAKE

These are the tips I wish someone had given me when I first started cooking. Correct these common errors and you'll see a dramatic improvement in your culinary skills.

1.
NOT SEASONING PROPERLY

Food tastes amazing at restaurants because chefs season generously and at the correct stage. Salt is the greatest flavour enhancer but if you just add it at the end you miss the opportunity to properly season your food from within. Unsalted cooking water will give you bland pasta, while green vegetables become grey and unappetising. Unsalted meat will not be as tender or as flavoursome, and you'll never achieve that crispy charred crust. No amount of seasoning at the table will fix these cooking errors. Use salt early in the cooking process to amplify flavour, soften proteins and enhance the natural sweetness of vegetables.

There are many gluten-free sources of salt beyond my much-loved sea salt flakes: fish sauce, tamari, coconut aminos, anchovies and miso paste all add a beautiful salty kick, along with their own unique flavour notes. Whole spices, peppercorns, bay leaves and cinnamon sticks will infuse your cooking liquid with aromatic notes and add complexity to your dishes. And don't forget a sprinkling of fresh herbs at the final stage to brighten your dish.

2.
FLAT FOOD

If your food tastes flat it is probably lacking acid. A little squeeze of lemon juice or a splash of vinegar will bring it to life and make the rest of the flavours 'pop'. Acid not only brightens food, it also tenderises proteins by helping to break down the collagen in slow-cooked meat.

Cooking acid mainly comes in the form of citrus juice, vinegar, wine, tomatoes and yoghurt. Garnishing acids can often be used interchangeably; for example, if you don't have a lemon for your salad dressing replace it with red or white wine vinegar – it will taste just as delicious.

3.
COLD INGREDIENTS

Ingredients emulsify better and food cooks more evenly if brought to room temperature first.

When baking, room-temperature ingredients, such as eggs and butter, incorporate more uniformly than cold ones (with the exception of pastry, which requires cold butter so it doesn't melt into the dough). Your cakes will be fluffier, your icing will be smoother and your cookies will be crispier.

When making sauces, room-temperature eggs emulsify better so your avgolemono (lemon–egg) sauce won't scramble and your mayonnaise is less likely to split.

Let your proteins sit at room temperature for at least 30 minutes prior to cooking for juicier steaks and chicken that is evenly cooked all the way through.

4.
OVERCROWDED PAN

We often cook in a rush so it is tempting to just throw everything in at once to speed up the process. Beware! Overcrowding the pan will steam your food, making it soggy and pale instead of crisp and caramelised. Your pan needs adequate heat distribution and surface area to brown and crisp your proteins and veggies correctly. If you need to sear a large quantity of meat do it in batches so you get an even colour all over. Colour equals flavour. When braising, remember to always return the resting juices from the cooked meat to the pan for extra flavour.

5.
OVERCOOKED INGREDIENTS

Overcooked veggies become soggy and limp and overcooked meat will be dry and tough.

You want to maintain crunchy texture and brightness in your veggies so don't overboil them. Overcooking will also lead to greater nutrient loss, so remember to keep it short and sharp.

Meat will continue to cook while it is resting so bear this in mind when timing your steak on the grill – it's probably best to pull it off a minute earlier rather than later.

NOT PROPERLY RESTING MEAT

Resting meat after cooking relaxes the muscle fibres and allows the juices to run back into the meat for a juicier and more flavoursome result. If you cut into a steak that has not rested properly the juices will run out onto your plate, leaving the meat dry and bland. As a general rule, the resting time should be half the cooking time, so if you cooked your steak for 6 minutes rest it for 3 minutes.

BURNT GARLIC

Because garlic burns easily it only needs around 30 seconds in the pan. Onions, celery and carrots (a common flavour base called mirepoix) are denser vegetables so they need more time to soften and caramelise. Cook the mirepoix before adding the garlic. A good tip to prevent burning vegetables before adding the garlic is to sprinkle them with sea salt to release their moisture and enhance their natural sweetness.

SOGGY (NOT CRISPY) SKIN

Moisture is the enemy of crispy skin. If you want crunchy pork crackling or crispy chicken and salmon skin remove as much moisture as possible by patting the skin dry with paper towel prior to cooking. If you have time, place meat or fish uncovered in the fridge overnight to air-dry the skin. A quick hack is to use your hairdryer to blow cold air all over the skin to help remove the moisture.

NOT ENOUGH QUALITY FAT

As well as being a vital cooking medium, quality fats, such as extra-virgin olive oil and coconut oil, play a role in flavouring food and achieving the correct texture. Fat contributes to the moistness of a cake, richness of a soup, silkiness of a sauce and juiciness of a one-pot braise. And if your pan does not have enough oil in it you will never achieve that perfect crispy crust on your steak.

I primarily cook with olive and coconut oils, but I also use avocado, macadamia, peanut and roasted sesame oils.

NOT PREPPING BEFORE YOU COOK

Make sure you have all your ingredients measured, cut, peeled and sliced before you start cooking. This is particularly important when stir-frying because once the wok is hot you need to move very quickly to avoid overcooking your food. Prepping is also a great way to spot missing ingredients so you have time to make a quick dash to the grocery store if need be. You can also arrange them on the bench to match the steps in the method so you don't miss anything.

NOT TASTING AS YOU GO

How will you know if your flavours need balancing if you don't taste as you go? Your braise may be lacking seasoning, for example, and if you don't correct it early enough you will miss your opportunity to properly infuse your braising liquid with aromats, to season the food from within. You also need to check that different components of your dish work together, so grab a little of everything on a fork to see if the flavours and textures combine well. And remember, always taste the final dish before you serve it!

THE GLUTEN-FREE KITCHEN

These are my essentials for a well-stocked gluten-free kitchen. With a diverse range of key ingredients on hand you can easily whip up a nourishing family meal any time of the day.

DARK (70% COCOA) CHOCOLATE
This is what I bake with when I want a rich chocolate flavour. A lower cocoa content will deliver a sweeter, less intense cocoa flavour and you will immediately notice the difference. Check the label to ensure there is no barley in the ingredients list because it contains gluten.

RAW CACAO AND COCOA POWDER
Raw cacao is made from cold-pressed unroasted cacao beans so it has incredible nutritional value, with high levels of magnesium and antioxidants. It is the extra-virgin olive oil of cocoa powders and the one I bake with most often. Cocoa powder is raw cacao that has been roasted at a high temperature. It comes in two forms: natural or dutch-process. Natural cocoa is light and bitter, whereas dutch-processed cocoa has been alkalised to deliver a deeper colour and a more mellow flavour – ideal when you want an intensely dark colour in your cakes or cookies.

COCONUT
I cook with coconut extensively in all its forms – milk, cream, desiccated, shredded and flaked. It is one of the most versatile foods in a gluten-free kitchen and brilliant in dairy-free recipes. I regularly use coconut milk and cream to replace dairy in dishes, such as my snapper pies (page 155) and crowd-pleasing coconut tiramisu (page 254). I find organic desiccated and shredded coconut to be far superior to non-organic brands in terms of taste, texture, moisture and aroma and well worth paying a little extra for.

COOKING SAUCES & VINEGARS

COCONUT AMINOS

Coconut aminos is a fantastic soy-free alternative to tamari, ideal for people who follow a soy-free diet. It is made from the fermented sap of a coconut palm and has the same salty umami notes of tamari with a milder, sweeter flavour.

DRY SHERRY

Chinese cooking wine (Shaoxing) is an aromatic wine commonly used in stir-fries but most people are unaware that wheat is sometimes used in the fermentation process. Dry sherry is a fantastic substitute, and you can pick up a bottle cheaply at any liquor store.

FISH, HOISIN AND OYSTER SAUCE

Premium brands of Asian sauces tend to be gluten free, but cheaper varieties often contain wheat and other fillers so always check the label. If you can't read the ingredients list on an Asian sauce bottle, don't buy it.

MISO PASTE

Miso is a rich Japanese fermented paste made primarily from soy beans. While most brands of miso are gluten free, some do contain wheat and barley so always check the label. If you don't eat soy choose a chickpea miso paste, which is soy free and just as delicious.

TAMARI

Most people are surprised to discover that soy sauce contains wheat starch. Tamari is a gluten-free soy sauce made without wheat starch, with a richer, deeper flavour than regular soy. While most tamari is wheat free, there are some that do contain wheat so always check the label carefully.

VINEGARS

Apple cider vinegar is the healthiest vinegar on the market. It contains amino acids, potassium and antioxidants so I always have plenty in my pantry for salad dressings. Other vinegars I use regularly include aged balsamic, sherry, and red and white wine vinegar.

FLOURS

Gluten-free flours generally fall into three categories:

- **Neutral white flours for bulk and starch:** rice flour, sweet rice flour, potato starch flour, tapioca flour and cornflour.
- **Nut meals/flours for protein, moisture, vitamins and minerals:** almond meal, hazelnut meal and chestnut flour.
- **Wholesome flours for protein and fibre:** chickpea (besan) flour, buckwheat flour, sorghum flour, teff flour, millet flour, tiger nut flour and quinoa flour.

If you suffer from additional allergies and need to substitute flours I suggest you do this within the same category. For example, if you have a rice allergy you can replace rice flour with another neutral white sticky flour such as tapioca. In the wholesome, nutrient-dense category, sorghum and buckwheat can be used interchangeably. The gluten-free flours I most commonly use are listed below.

BUCKWHEAT

Despite the name buckwheat is a seed and does not contain any wheat. Nutritionally dense, it is high in protein, fibre, iron, zinc, selenium and B vitamins plus it can also aid digestion. Buckwheat has an earthy flavour and soft starchy texture so it's perfect in breads and pancakes. If you want to mellow its assertive flavour, blend it with a neutral white flour, such as sweet rice or tapioca.

CHICKPEA (BESAN) FLOUR

Made from ground chickpeas this flour has a mild, nutty taste. It is fantastic in savoury dishes, such as socca (see page 38), pancakes and fritters, because its sticky texture gives it great binding qualities, ideal when working sans gluten. It is high in protein, fibre, antioxidants and micronutrients, making it one of the healthiest flours you can keep in your pantry.

CORNFLOUR

Cornflour is a fine white flour derived from ground corn kernels. It's a great binder and has a neutral flavour so it's extremely versatile in pastry making. Make sure you purchase a brand made from 100 per cent corn and labelled 'gluten free' because some brands contain wheat.

GLUTEN-FREE PLAIN (ALL-PURPOSE) FLOUR

The quality of commercial gluten-free plain flours can vary greatly. Every manufacturer has their own unique blend, aiming to mimic regular wheat flour. Some brands bake well while others will leave you with a crumbly mess. My advice is to try a few before you settle on one you like. As a general rule you get what you pay for, with the more expensive brands delivering far superior results.

NUT AND SEED MEALS

Nut meals are made from ground nuts, such as almonds, hazelnuts and pistachios. They have a slightly coarse texture and rich, nutty flavour. Nut meals are high in protein, fibre, vitamins, minerals and healthy fats, making them a great option for people following a low-carb, grain-free or paleo diet. The natural fats add incredible moistness and richness to food, quite often meaning the recipe doesn't require added fat. For example, my simple chocolate & hazelnut cake on page 258 stays wonderfully moist from hazelnut meal alone. If you have a nut allergy, seed meals, such as pumpkin or sunflower can be used as a substitute.

SORGHUM

Sorghum is a nutrition powerhouse that is high in antioxidants, protein, fibre and iron, with a smooth texture and mild sweet taste. It pairs well with neutral white flours to add great flavour, texture and nutritional value to baked goods. Do note that it has a bitter profile so I generally don't use more than 30 per cent sorghum in a flour blend.

POTATO STARCH

Potato starch (or potato starch flour) is made from the dried starch component of peeled potatoes, and it adds softness and lightness to gluten-free baked goods. It is not the same as potato flour and you cannot substitute one for the other. Potato flour is made from whole potatoes, has a heavy texture and strong potato flavour. I never use it.

TAPIOCA

The most versatile flour in the gluten-free pantry is tapioca, derived from the cassava plant native to South America. Tapioca is great for binding, thickening and crumbing, and adds great texture to baked goods. It will make your bread bouncy, your crumb light and your sauces thicker.

TIGER NUT FLOUR

Tiger nuts are not actually nuts, they are a root vegetable with a sweet, nutty flavour. Tiger nut flour is extremely versatile and can be used as a nut-free alternative to almond meal, providing moistness and a delicate sweetness to baked goods. This ground root flour is very high in dietary fibre and resistant starch so it is great for gut health. It is also a good source of iron, potassium, protein, magnesium, zinc and vitamins C and E.

XANTHAN GUM

Xanthan gum is used as a thickening substitute in gluten-free baking. It mimics the qualities of gluten and helps baked goods rise by trapping air bubbles created by leavening agents such as baking powder and yeast. If you are sensitive to xanthan gum you can replace it with psyllium husks or ground chia seeds to add some elasticity to your recipes.

GRAINS & PSEUDOGRAINS

BUCKWHEAT

Buckwheat seeds (also called groats or kernels) have a triangular shape and are high in protein, antioxidants and essential amino acids. They can be cooked like rice and used in salads and sides. Raw buckwheat seeds that have been soaked and dehydrated are called buckinis (or raw activated buckwheat). Buckinis have a super crunchy texture so they are fantastic in raw vegan desserts and breakfast cereals, and make a delicious crunchy garnish on yoghurt and smoothie bowls.

GLUTEN-FREE PASTA

There are many great brands of gluten-free pasta on the market, made primarily from a blend of corn, rice, potato and tapioca. You can also buy high-fibre and high-protein gluten-free pulse pastas made with peas, chickpeas, beans and lentils. Whatever your preference, remember to cook your pasta in a saucepan of salted boiling water until just al dente so it doesn't become too mushy. Drag some starchy pasta water into your sauces to make them silkier and help the sauce cling to the pasta. Pair rich sauces, such as bolognese, with wider, chunkier shapes that can stand up to the sauce, and delicate shapes, such as angel hair spaghetti, with lighter sauces.

POLENTA

Polenta is a versatile gluten-free grain made from corn. It can be served hot as a porridge or cooled into a solid slab for baking, grilling or frying. Polenta can also be used for crumbing or baking polenta cakes. It is sold in two forms: regular and instant. Regular polenta cooks in about 40 minutes and requires frequent stirring, while instant polenta can be whisked together in a few minutes. Instant wins in terms of convenience, but for creaminess and flavour regular polenta is superior.

QUINOA

Quinoa is one of the most versatile and nutrient-dense 'superfoods' in a gluten-free pantry. Technically a seed, it is referred to as a 'pseudograin' because it is generally cooked and eaten like a cereal grain. Quinoa is a complete protein containing all nine essential amino acids and it is also high in protein, fibre, magnesium, iron, potassium and antioxidants. Quinoa must be thoroughly rinsed before cooking to remove its natural saponin coating, which has a bitter taste and can be difficult to digest.

Quinoa is sold in three different forms:

- **Quinoa seeds** are light and fluffy when cooked so they are a fantastic nutrient-dense replacement for couscous, rice and pasta. I serve braised dishes like Moroccan lamb tajine (page 216) and glazed lamb shanks (page 222) on a bed of fluffy quinoa to mop up the sauce. They are also a great addition to salads for a wholesome lunch (see my quinoa & herb salad on page 52).
- **Quinoa flakes** are pressed quinoa seeds so they cook in a fraction of the time – perfect for busy mornings when you want to whip up a bowl of creamy porridge (see page 26). Quinoa flakes can also be used cup for cup as a substitute for oats in toasted granolas, muesli bars and cookies, and are a nutrient-dense crumbing option in dishes like the crumbed chicken on page 170.
- **Quinoa flour** is a great way to boost the nutrition profile of flour when baking. Replace up to half of your plain flour with quinoa for a protein, fibre and antioxidant boost.

RICE

All rice is naturally gluten free, whether it is white, brown, wild, arborio or glutinous rice. 'Glutinous' rice does not contain gluten – the name refers to the sticky nature of the rice due to its high starch content. Rice noodles are a great alternative to wheat-based egg noodles in Asian stir-fries. When you're eating out, ask to swap wheat-based egg noodles for rice vermicelli or wide rice noodles like those in pad thai.

SOBA NOODLES

These Japanese buckwheat noodles have a slightly nutty taste and are a great source of protein, fibre, thiamin and manganese. When eating lean and clean, soba noodles are a great carb option in dishes like my sesame-crusted cod with soba noodles (page 167). They are either made with 100 per cent buckwheat flour or a blend of buckwheat and wheat flour, so check the packet and make sure you buy the former.

HERBS & SPICES

Fresh and dried herbs and spices are not only a healthy way to flavour your food, they are also nutrient dense and anti-inflammatory. These are my favourites.

FRESH	DRIED
basil	allspice
bay leaf	cinnamon
coriander	coriander
dill	cumin
flat-leaf parsley	fennel
mint	nutmeg
oregano	oregano
rosemary	pepper (ground white and black)
sage	sea salt flakes
tarragon	star anise
thyme	sumac

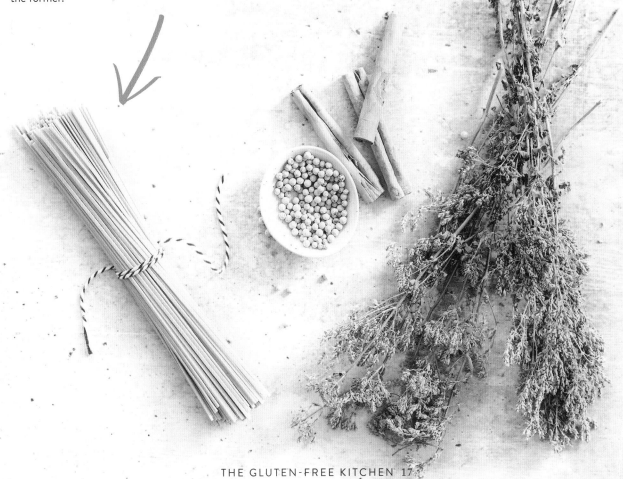

OILS, FATS & EGGS

COCONUT OIL

Coconut oil is extracted from the meat of mature coconuts. It is high in medium-chain triglycerides (MCTs), which are metabolised differently from other fats, providing a sustained energy source. The fatty acids in coconut oil may boost good cholesterol (HDL). Coconut oil has a high smoke point so it can be used for stir-frying, and it's a great dairy-free substitute in baking.

OTHER NATURAL OILS

I also cook with avocado oil, macadamia oil, peanut oil and toasted sesame oil. I prefer oils that are made naturally by pressing or crushing a seed over highly refined vegetable oils extracted using chemical solvents. Refined oils can be high in trans fatty acids, which can increase bad cholesterol levels.

ORGANIC EGGS

I use large organic eggs (55 g) in my recipes.

EXTRA-VIRGIN OLIVE OIL

Extra-virgin olive oil forms the foundation of my cooking. 'Extra virgin' is the first cold-pressed oil derived from the olive, retaining the most health benefits as well as an intense olive flavour. Contrary to popular belief, you can actually fry with a good-quality extra-virgin olive oil – just don't overheat the pan. Extra-virgin olive oil has a smoke point of 200–210°C, which is above the 180°C required for deep-frying. Light extra-virgin olive oil is further refined so it has a mild, delicate flavour and is more suited to baking or mayonnaises when you don't want an overt olive taste.

ORGANIC BUTTER

I don't cook with butter often. I mainly use it when baking and for sauces like bechamel. I prefer organic butter as I find it has a creamier texture and smoother flavour than non-organic varieties.

MEAT & SEAFOOD

When it comes to animal proteins I always look for organic, grass-fed meat free of pesticides and chemicals. Organic chicken meat is moister and more flavoursome than non-organic, and grass-fed red meat is higher in certain vitamins and healthy fats, like omega 3, than grain-fed meat.

When buying seafood 'wild caught' is the healthier option. It has fewer toxins and chemicals because the fish feed on a diet of smaller fish and algae in their natural habitat. Overall, organic and wild-caught proteins are more expensive but they taste far superior and are better for you. If you can't afford these options just purchase the best-quality proteins you can.

SWEETENERS

MAPLE SYRUP

Only buy 100 per cent pure maple syrup made from evaporated tree sap, not the imitation syrup with additives. Real maple syrup is rich in antioxidants, zinc, magnesium, calcium and potassium, and has a richer, purer flavour than the imitations. Maple syrup also has antibacterial and anti-inflammatory properties.

NUTS & SEEDS

Where possible I purchase activated nuts and seeds because I love their crunchy texture and digestive benefits. Activated nuts have been soaked in salted water and then dehydrated to increase their nutritional value and to make them easier to digest. Always check the label to ensure shelled nuts and seeds, such as pistachios and pumpkin seeds, have not been dusted in flour. This has caught me out a few times!

MEDJOOL DATES

Medjool dates are often referred to as nature's caramel. They have a soft chewy texture and richer taste compared to regular dates, which are smaller, firmer and less flavoursome. Because medjool dates are a fresh fruit you'll find them with the fresh produce rather than in the dried fruit section of the grocery store. They are high in potassium, magnesium, iron and other vitamins and minerals.

RAW HONEY

Raw honey is unprocessed and not heat treated so you get a pure, full-bodied honey that retains beneficial antioxidant and nutritional properties, such as vitamin B6, zinc and potassium. Pasteurisation and heating reduces the anti-fungal and antibacterial properties of honey so it is worth paying a little extra for a raw variety.

WHAT ABOUT SUGAR?

In the sweet chapter I have included recipes containing cane sugar, which I consume in moderation, primarily when baking. If you do not wish to bake with refined sugar, great unrefined alternatives (apart from those already listed) are coconut sugar and rapadura. Both have beautiful caramel notes, a small amount of minerals and a lower glycemic index (GI) than cane sugar.

GLUTEN-FREE GRAIN & SEED COOKING GUIDE

GRAIN	METHOD	YIELD
Buckwheat kernels	Rinse 180 g (1 cup) buckwheat kernels under cold running water and place in a saucepan with 500 ml (2 cups) water. Bring to the boil, then reduce the heat and simmer, covered, for 8 minutes or until tender. Drain.	2¼ cups cooked buckwheat
Buckwheat soba noodles	Add 400 g soba noodles to a large saucepan of boiling water and cook for 6 minutes. Drain and rinse thoroughly under cold water, separating the noodles with your hands.	Serves 4 people
Polenta (instant)	Bring 1 litre water or gluten-free stock to the boil in a saucepan. Remove the pan from the heat. Whisk in 150 g (1 cup) instant polenta and stir for 1 minute until it thickens. Stir in 2 teaspoons sea salt flakes and 40 g butter (or extra-virgin olive oil for a dairy-free version) until melted and combined.	3 cups creamy polenta
Rice (basmati, jasmine, medium-grain, sushi and short-grain)	**Absorption Method** Rinse 200 g (1 cup) rice under cold running water and place in a saucepan with 375 ml (1½ cups) water. Bring to the boil, then reduce the heat to low and simmer, covered, for 15 minutes. Remove from the heat and let and stand with the lid on for another 5 minutes. **Boiling Method** Rinse 200 g (1 cup) rice under cold running water and place in a saucepan with 2 litres cold water. Bring to the boil, stirring occasionally, then reduce the heat to low and simmer, covered, for 15 minutes. Drain well.	3 cups cooked rice
Quinoa	Rinse 200 g (1 cup) quinoa under cold running water and place in a small saucepan with 500 ml (2 cups) water. Simmer, covered, over low heat for 10 minutes. Remove from the heat and cool with the lid on, then fluff with a fork.	3 cups cooked quinoa
Quinoa flakes	Rinse 50 g (⅓ cup) quinoa flakes under cold running water and place in a small saucepan with 250 ml (1 cup) of your preferred milk. Simmer over low heat, stirring regularly, for 1–2 minutes or until your desired consistency is achieved.	1 cup creamy porridge

BREAKFAST & BAKERY

The Fluffiest Pancakes
EVER

SERVES 2–4   DF, GF, V

Rise and shine to the easiest pancakes you will ever make. All you need is a bowl and spoon and you can whip up a batch in minutes. Coconut milk works beautifully in pancakes – they turn out extra moist and fluffy and, in case it's an issue, you can't taste the coconut at all. If you prefer to use regular or almond milk, go right ahead. I love a classic topping of banana, cinnamon and maple syrup but you can be as creative as you like with your garnishes and drizzles.

170 g (1⅓ cups) plain gluten-free flour, sifted
1 tablespoon gluten-free baking powder
3 tablespoons caster sugar
pinch of sea salt flakes
250 ml (1 cup) coconut milk (or milk of
   your choice), plus extra if needed
1 egg, whisked
2 teaspoons vanilla extract
1 tablespoon melted coconut oil, plus extra
   for pan-frying
pure maple syrup, blueberries and mint,
   to serve

Whisk together the flour, baking powder, sugar and salt in a bowl. Add the milk, egg, vanilla and coconut oil and whisk to form a thick, smooth batter. Add extra milk if the batter is too thick.

Heat a non-stick frying pan over medium heat and melt a little extra coconut oil. Add a ladleful of batter and cook until bubbles appear on the surface. Flip over and cook for another minute.

Repeat with the remaining batter, adding a little more coconut oil when needed.

Serve with your favourite toppings.

VARIATION
- Give your pancakes a nutritious fibre boost by replacing 50 g (⅓ cup) plain gluten-free flour with 30 g (⅓ cup) tiger nut flour.

Speedy Quinoa & CHIA PORRIDGE

SERVES 2 DF, GF, VG

I don't know what mornings are like at your place but at my house it is utter chaos. I only have a few minutes to get breakfast on the table before the kids rush off to school, so I want to feed them something healthy that ticks all the boxes: easy, quick, nutrient dense and high protein to keep them full until lunchtime. Quinoa flakes cook in a fraction of the time regular quinoa seeds take so they are perfect for a creamy bowl of gluten-free porridge. Give them a go – they are so easy to cook with!

45 g (⅓ cup) quinoa flakes
250 ml (1 cup) milk (any kind), plus extra
   if needed
2 tablespoons white chia seeds
1 tablespoon pure maple syrup or raw honey
½ teaspoon ground cinnamon
your choice of fruit, nuts and coconut flakes,
   to serve

Place the quinoa flakes in a sieve and rinse under running water to remove any bitterness.

Tip the flakes into a saucepan, add the milk, chia seeds, maple syrup or honey and cinnamon and simmer over low heat for 1 minute or until the porridge reaches your desired consistency. If you prefer it thinner add extra milk, and for a thicker consistency simmer for a minute or two longer.

Spoon the porridge into bowls and garnish with your favourite toppings.

NOTE
- Quinoa flakes are simply pressed quinoa seeds. They cook much faster but offer the same nutritional benefits.

Easy Bowl & Spoon
GLUTEN-FREE LOAF

MAKES 1 LOAF   DF, GF, V

Baking doesn't get much easier than this. Unlike regular bread, which requires kneading, all you need to do with this loaf is mix the ingredients in a bowl like a cake batter, then pour into a tin for a light, fluffy loaf (not dense and heavy, as gluten-free bread can often be). Tapioca is fantastic in gluten-free bread because it gives it a soft, bouncy texture, and buckwheat injects a nutritious boost of protein, fibre and antioxidants. Get creative and replace the sesame seeds with chia seeds, poppy seeds, linseeds or pumpkin seeds, or you could even go seedless. All combinations are delicious!

1 teaspoon caster sugar
7 g sachet dried yeast
2 eggs
3 tablespoons extra-virgin olive oil,
    plus extra for drizzling
1 teaspoon apple cider vinegar
210 g (1¾ cups) tapioca flour, sifted
210 g (1¾ cups) buckwheat flour, sifted
2 teaspoons sea salt flakes
½ teaspoon xanthan gum
sesame seeds, for sprinkling

Place the sugar, yeast and 300 ml of lukewarm water in a jug and whisk to combine. Leave to stand for 10–15 minutes or until the mixture foams.

Whisk the eggs in a separate bowl, then stir in the olive oil and vinegar.

Combine the flours, salt and xanthan gum in a large bowl and make a well in the centre. Pour the yeast and egg mixtures into the well and mix with a spoon until well combined.

Grease a 20 cm × 10 cm loaf tin with olive oil and sprinkle sesame seeds on the base and sides to create a seeded crust. Spoon the dough into the tin and cover with plastic wrap. Place in a warm place for about 1 hour or until the dough has almost doubled in size.

Meanwhile, preheat the oven to 200°C (fan-forced).

Drizzle olive oil over the risen dough and sprinkle with sesame seeds. Bake for 45 minutes or until golden. Remove the tin from the oven and immediately transfer the bread to a wire rack to cool (this will help the crust stay crisp). Leave to cool for a few hours before slicing.

The loaf will keep in an airtight container at room temperature for 3 days or in the fridge for 1 week. Alternatively, slice it and freeze for up to a month. Frozen slices toast well – no thawing required.

TIP
- Don't slice the bread while it's still hot as it will be gummy and sticky. You need to let the steam inside settle for a few hours first.

VARIATION
- Replace the buckwheat flour with tiger nut flour for a slightly sweeter loaf that is equally nutritious.

Soft Greek
PITA BREADS

MAKES 4   DF, GF, VG

I eat yeeros (see page 196) quite often so I developed a recipe for gluten-free pita bread that was soft, light and flexible enough to wrap around fillings. It's super versatile and easy to make so you never have to settle for an inferior store-bought version again. The key is to roll the dough thinly between two sheets of baking paper before transferring to a very hot frying pan. The result is golden, puffy pita with crispy edges that your friends and family would never guess is gluten free!

½ teaspoon caster sugar
1 teaspoon dried yeast
195 g (1½ cups) plain gluten-free flour
1 teaspoon sea salt flakes
1 tablespoon extra-virgin olive oil, plus extra
  for drizzling

Place the sugar, yeast and 180 ml (¾ cup) of lukewarm water in a jug and whisk to combine. Leave to stand for 10–15 minutes or until the mixture foams.

Place the flour in the bowl of an electric mixer fitted with the dough hook and crush in the salt flakes with your fingers. Pour in the yeast mixture and olive oil and mix for about 1 minute to form a ball.

Place the dough in a clean, greased bowl, cover with plastic wrap and rest for 1 hour or until it doubles in size. (If you are making this ahead, the dough will keep in the fridge for up to 3 days.)

Divide the dough into four even portions and roll into balls. Working with one ball at a time, drizzle over a little olive oil and massage to coat. Place the dough between two sheets of baking paper and roll out to a thin 20 cm round.

Heat a cast-iron frying pan over high heat and drizzle with a little olive oil. Remove the top layer of baking paper, then flip the dough round onto the hot pan and peel away the remaining baking paper. Cook for 2–3 minutes on each side until golden and puffy. Remove and cover with a tea towel to keep warm while you cook the rest.

Quick Yoghurt Flatbreads
WITH BEETROOT DIP

SERVES 4–6   GF, V

These versatile flatbreads only require a few pantry staples and no resting time, so you can have them ready in a flash to scoop up dips, soups and curries. The addition of a whisked egg helps to bind the dough and make it more pliable – my little gluten-free trick! The combination of sweet and savoury ingredients in the beetroot dip packs a flavour punch and its vibrant colour immediately attracts attention. This is the prettiest starter or snack for entertaining.

130 g (1 cup) plain gluten-free flour
2 teaspoons gluten-free baking powder
pinch of sea salt flakes
3 tablespoons Greek yoghurt
3 tablespoons extra-virgin olive oil, plus extra
   for brushing
1 egg, lightly whisked

BEETROOT DIP

2 large beetroot, peeled and cubed
100 ml extra-virgin olive oil
1 tablespoon balsamic vinegar
1 tablespoon raw honey
1 tablespoon chopped rosemary or thyme
   leaves, plus extra sprigs to serve
50 g (½ cup) walnuts
pinch of sea salt flakes and freshly ground
   black pepper

To make the dip, steam the beetroot in a steaming basket over simmering water for 15–20 minutes until tender. Place the beetroot in a blender, add the remaining ingredients and blitz to a smooth paste. Taste and adjust the seasoning if necessary. Store in an airtight container in the fridge for up to 3 days.

Combine the flour, baking powder and salt in a bowl. Add the yoghurt, olive oil and egg and mix with your hands to form a pliable dough.

Divide the dough into four even portions and roll into balls. Working with one ball at a time, place the dough between two sheets of baking paper and roll out to a thin oval shape about 20 cm long. Remove the top layer of baking paper and brush the dough with a little extra olive oil.

Heat a chargrill pan over high heat. Using your baking paper, flip the dough round onto the hot pan and peel away the paper. Cook for 2–3 minutes on each side until charred and golden. Remove and cover with a tea towel to keep warm while you cook the rest.

Serve the flatbreads with the beetroot dip and sprinkle over some rosemary or thyme leaves before serving.

NOTE
• Beetroot is high in vitamin C, fibre and essential minerals, such as potassium and magnesium, making this is a nutrient-dense dip.

Tiropites
(ROUGH PUFF CHEESE PIES)

MAKES 16   GF, V

Making pastry can be daunting for any home cook; add the gluten-free element and most people run in fear. Do not despair, I have a fantastic rough puff pastry recipe that is light and flaky and far superior to the gluggy, heavily processed packaged gluten-free options. I really missed tiropites when I cut out gluten and I am delighted to welcome these pastry pillows oozing with warm feta and ricotta back into my life. Tiropites freeze well so they are great for morning teas and lunchboxes – just remember to extend the cooking time by about 10 minutes if baking from frozen.

1 egg, lightly whisked, for brushing
sesame seeds, for sprinkling (optional)

ROUGH PUFF PASTRY
125 g (1 cup) gluten-free cornflour
120 g (¾ cup) potato starch
70 g (½ cup) sorghum flour
2 teaspoons xanthan gum
1 teaspoon sea salt flakes
250 g very cold butter, cubed
1 egg

CHEESE FILLING
300 g full-fat ricotta
200 g Greek feta, crumbled
1 egg, whisked
1 teaspoon sea salt flakes
pinch of ground white pepper

To make the rough puff pastry, place the cornflour, potato starch, sorghum flour, xanthan gum and salt in a food processor and pulse to combine. Add the butter and egg and pulse until the mixture resembles breadcrumbs. Mix in 1–2 tablespoons of cold water – just enough to form a rubble.

Tip the rubble onto a sheet of baking paper and press with floured hands into a rectangle. Place another sheet of baking paper on top and roll out the dough to a larger rectangle – you still want to see streaks of butter. Fold in the short edges to meet in the middle, then fold the pastry in half. Wrap in plastic wrap and rest in the fridge for 30 minutes. Repeat the roll, fold and rest routine twice more. If your dough is too sticky, dust it with a little extra cornflour or chill for longer to firm it up.

To make the cheese filling, place the ingredients in a bowl and mix well with your hands.

Preheat the oven to 200°C (fan-forced) and line a large baking tray with baking paper.

Remove the pastry from the fridge and cut into four even portions. You will be working with one portion at a time, so return the remaining pastry to the fridge so it stays cold. Roll out the pastry between two sheets of baking paper to produce a thin (1–2 mm) pastry sheet. Using a 12 cm round cutter or small plate, cut out rounds of pastry. Place 2 tablespoons of filling on one side of each round, brush the edge with beaten egg, then fold over the pastry and seal with your fingers to create a pillow. Repeat with the remaining pastry.

Brush the pastries with the remaining beaten egg and sprinkle with sesame seeds (if using). Place on the prepared tray and bake for 30–35 minutes until golden.

VARIATION
• To make spanakopita, add a large handful of chopped silverbeet, 2 tablespoons of chopped dill fronds and 2 sliced spring onions to the cheese filling.

Leek & Mushroom Tart
IN SHORTCRUST PASTRY

SERVES 8   GF, V

Vegetarian tarts are a fantastic option if you're having people over for morning tea or lunch as they look really fancy and are satisfying without being heavy. This impressive tart – a heavenly combination of mushrooms and leek infused with thyme and garlic – is very easy to make. The shortcrust pastry is beautifully crumbly and super versatile – it works so well with any number of fillings. You are only limited by your imagination.

3 tablespoons extra-virgin olive oil
1 leek, white and light green parts, washed and finely sliced
300 g mixed mushrooms, sliced
1 tablespoon chopped thyme leaves, plus extra to serve
pinch of sea salt flakes and freshly ground black pepper
2 eggs
125 ml (½ cup) milk
50 g kefalograviera cheese, manchego or sharp cheddar, grated, plus extra, shaved, for sprinkling (optional)

SHORTCRUST PASTRY
90 g (¾ cup) gluten-free cornflour
100 g (¾ cup) sweet rice flour (also known as glutinous rice flour)
50 g (⅓ cup) sorghum flour
35 g (⅓ cup) almond meal
1 tablespoon sea salt flakes
125 g cold unsalted butter, cut into cubes
1 egg

To make the pastry, place the flours, almond meal and salt in a food processor and pulse to combine. Add the butter and egg and pulse until the mixture resembles breadcrumbs. Mix in 2–3 tablespoons of cold water – just enough to form a rubble.

Tip the rubble onto a sheet of plastic wrap and bring it together with your hands to form a disc. Wrap tightly in plastic wrap and rest in the fridge for 1 hour. This will allow the flour to absorb the moisture, making it more pliable and less likely to shrink.

Preheat the oven to 180°C (fan-forced) and line the base of a rectangular tart tin (roughly 35 cm × 13 cm) with baking paper.

Roll out the pastry thinly between two sheets of baking paper. Carefully flip the pastry into the prepared tin and peel away the baking paper. Using your hands, gently press the pastry into the base and sides of the tin and roll over the edges to cut off the overhang. Line the pastry with baking paper and fill with baking beads or uncooked rice, then place in the oven and blind-bake for 15 minutes. Remove the paper and weights and set aside to cool for 10 minutes.

Heat the olive oil in a large frying pan over medium–high heat. Add the leek, mushroom, thyme, salt and pepper and sauté for 5 minutes or until softened. Spoon the mixture into the pastry case and spread it out evenly.

Whisk the eggs, milk and cheese in a bowl and pour evenly over the mushroom filling. If you like, shave over some extra cheese, then bake for 30 minutes or until golden. Sprinkle with extra cheese and thyme, to serve, if desired.

VARIATION
- To make a sweet shortcrust pastry, simply omit the salt and add 60 g (½ cup) of sifted gluten-free icing sugar. This is a fantastic pastry for galettes and sweet pies.

TIP
- Kefalograviera is a salty sheep's milk cheese that can be found in European delis and gourmet grocers.

Kale & Pea Socca
WITH YOGHURT–TAHINI SAUCE

SERVES 4   DF, GF, VG

Socca is a savoury chickpea pancake originating from the south of France. Chickpea flour adds earthiness and nutty notes to the pancake and it's also full of protein, fibre and micronutrients. You get a second superfood boost from the kale, peas and fresh herbs, and the creamy yoghurt–tahini sauce is delicious smothered on top. I have prepared the dressing with coconut yoghurt to keep the entire meal vegan but a natural Greek yoghurt works beautifully, too. Once you've mastered the basic batter you can season and fill it as you wish, so get creative!

extra-virgin olive oil, for pan-frying

SOCCA BATTER

140 g (1 cup) chickpea (besan) flour
1 teaspoon sea salt flakes
1 teaspoon ground cumin
1 tablespoon extra-virgin olive oil
115 g (¾ cup) fresh or frozen peas, plus extra
   cooked peas to serve
handful of kale leaves, finely sliced
2 tablespoons finely chopped coriander leaves,
   plus extra leaves to serve
2 tablespoons finely chopped mint leaves,
   plus extra leaves to serve
1 spring onion, finely sliced
1 teaspoon finely grated lemon zest

YOGHURT–TAHINI SAUCE

125 g (½ cup) coconut yoghurt
1 tablespoon tahini
1 tablespoon lemon juice
pinch of sea salt flakes and freshly ground
   black pepper

To make the socca batter, combine the flour, salt and cumin in a bowl and make a well in the centre. Pour in the olive oil and 250 ml (1 cup) of water and stir to combine. Add all the remaining ingredients and mix well.

Heat a little olive oil in a small non-stick frying pan over medium heat. Add one quarter of the batter and tilt to coat the base, then cook for 2–3 minutes each side until golden and crisp. Remove and cover with a tea towel to keep warm while you cook the rest.

To make the yoghurt–tahini sauce, whisk the ingredients in a bowl.

To serve, top each socca with the sauce and finish with extra peas, a good grinding of pepper and fresh herbs.

Cauliflower Pizza Base
3 WAYS

MAKES 1 LARGE PIZZA BASE   GF, LC, V

Grated cauliflower makes a fantastic pizza base that is not only gluten free but also low carb for a guilt-free pizza night. If you've attempted cauliflower pizza in the past and your base has fallen apart it's probably because there was too much moisture in your dough. The key is to squeeze your steamed cauliflower very firmly to release all the moisture. The pizza base is cooked in two stages – first you bake the cauliflower dough to form a crust, then you add your favourite toppings and bake a second time until crisp and golden.

1 small head of cauliflower (about 500 g),
   cut into florets
35 g (⅓ cup) finely grated parmesan
1–2 eggs, lightly whisked
pinch of sea salt flakes and ground
   white pepper

Preheat the oven to 200°C (fan-forced) and line a 30 cm round pizza tray with baking paper.

Blitz the cauliflower in a food processor until it resembles rice. Tip it into a glass bowl, cover with plastic wrap and microwave on high for 5 minutes.

Tip the warm cauliflower into a piece of muslin or cheese cloth over a bowl and cool for 15 minutes. Very firmly squeeze out all the water so the cauliflower is completely dry.

Combine the cauliflower, cheese, egg, salt and pepper in a clean bowl. Place the mixture on the prepared tray and cover with another sheet of baking paper. Using a spatula, firmly spread the mixture (still covered in baking paper) to form a smooth, even base. Peel away the top sheet of paper and bake for 15 minutes. Remove from the oven, flip the base onto a new tray and peel away the baking paper.

Now all you need to do is choose a topping.

MARGARITA
- Combine 125 ml (½ cup) passata, ¼ teaspoon dried oregano and 1 crushed garlic clove and spread over the pizza base. Sprinkle with a generous handful of grated mozzarella and bake for 10 minutes or until golden.

PROSCIUTTO & ROCKET (PICTURED)
- Follow the steps for margarita above, and either arrange 6–8 slices of prosciutto over the cheese prior to baking or add after cooking. Remove the pizza from the oven and top with sliced pear and a handful of rocket leaves.

BARBECUE CHICKEN
- Top the pizza base with 125 ml (½ cup) gluten-free barbecue sauce, 175 g (1 cup) shredded cooked chicken, ½ finely sliced red onion, and 150 g (1 cup) grated mozzarella. Bake for 10 minutes or until golden. Garnish with coriander leaves and serve.

Thai Chicken Sausage Rolls
WITH LIME & SWEET CHILLI DIPPING SAUCE

MAKES 18   GF

Sausage rolls are always a hit at parties so I make them in bulk and freeze for an easy entertaining option or afternoon snack. This is a delicious Thai take on an Aussie classic and the lime and sweet chilli dipping sauce is the perfect zesty accompaniment. I have kept the spice level mild so they are kid friendly, but if you like a bit of heat add another tablespoon or two of curry paste.

2 x quantity Rough Puff Pastry (page 35)
beaten egg, for brushing
sesame seeds, for sprinkling

FILLING
500 g chicken thigh mince
2 tablespoons gluten-free Thai red curry paste
1 tablespoon fish sauce
1 large carrot, peeled and finely grated, excess
    moisture squeezed out
2 garlic cloves, finely grated
2 teaspoons finely grated ginger
2 spring onions, finely chopped
2 tablespoons finely chopped coriander leaves
1 egg

LIME & SWEET CHILLI DIPPING SAUCE
3 tablespoons gluten-free sweet chilli sauce
finely grated zest of ½ lime
juice of 1 lime
½ teaspoon finely grated ginger

Preheat the oven to 200°C (fan-forced) and line a large baking tray with baking paper.

To make the filling, place all ingredients in a food processor and blitz until well combined.

Divide the pastry into three portions. You will be working with one portion at a time, so return the remaining pastry to the fridge so it stays cold. Place one portion of pastry between two sheets of baking paper and roll it out into a rectangle roughly 30 cm long and 12 cm wide. The thinner the pastry, the flakier it will be. If it tears, just pinch it together with your fingers.

Place one-third of the sausage filling along the length of the pastry rectangle. Brush the long edge closest to you with beaten egg, then roll over to enclose the filling and seal. Brush the top of the pastry with egg and sprinkle with sesame seeds. Repeat with the remaining two pieces. Cut each roll at 5 cm intervals to make 18 sausage rolls.

Place the rolls on the prepared tray, seam-side down. Bake for 30 minutes or until the filling is cooked through and the pastry is golden.

Meanwhile, to make the sauce, combine the ingredients in a small bowl. Serve with the warm sausage rolls.

SALADS

Roasted Miso Pumpkin
& ROCKET SALAD

SERVES 4   DF, GF, LC, V

I'm slightly obsessed with roasted pumpkin – it's one of the most versatile vegetables you can cook with. Roasting pumpkin intensifies its flavour and caramelises its natural sugars, resulting in a crispy golden exterior and honeyed flesh centre. The contrasting flavours and textures make this salad a showstopper – umami notes from the miso, sweetness from the pumpkin, bitterness from the rocket leaves and crunch from the toasted seeds. Even a die-hard carnivore will be converted!

3 tablespoons extra-virgin olive oil
1 tablespoon gluten-free white miso paste (see Tips)
sea salt flakes and freshly ground black pepper
600 g kent or butternut pumpkin, peeled and cut into 4 cm cubes (see Tips)
1 large red onion, cut into wedges
100 g rocket leaves
2 tablespoons pumpkin seeds
2 tablespoons toasted sesame seeds (see Tips)

DRESSING
3 tablespoons extra-virgin olive oil
1 garlic clove, finely grated
3 cm piece of ginger, finely grated
1 teaspoon gluten-free white miso paste
juice of 1 lime
sea salt flakes and freshly ground black pepper

Preheat the oven to 200°C (fan-forced) and line a baking tray with baking paper.

In a bowl, whisk together the olive oil, miso paste and a pinch of salt and pepper. Place the pumpkin and onion on the prepared tray, pour over the miso mixture and toss to coat. Roast for 30 minutes or until the pumpkin is soft, tossing halfway through to ensure even browning. Remove and allow to cool slightly.

Meanwhile, to make the dressing, whisk the ingredients in a bowl.

Place the rocket, warm pumpkin and onion in a bowl, pour over the dressing and toss well to combine. Transfer the salad to a platter, scatter over the pumpkin and sesame seeds and serve.

TIPS

- I generally use white miso paste, but if you have a soy allergy use chickpea miso instead.

- You can replace the pumpkin with sweet potato if preferred, or roast a combination of both.

- Toasting sesame seeds makes them super crunchy and nutty. To do this, just add them to a dry frying pan and cook over low heat for 2–3 minutes, swirling the pan regularly to prevent them burning.

Fennel, Haloumi
& POMEGRANATE SALAD

SERVES 4 GF, LC, V

Haloumi was a staple cheese in my household when I was growing up. My mother always served it chargrilled with a generous squeeze of lemon juice and a sprinkling of oregano. In this refreshing summer salad the squeaky texture and saltiness of the haloumi contrasts beautifully with the aniseed flavour of the crisp fennel and the sweet bursts of pomegranate juice from the antioxidant-rich seeds.

1 small fennel bulb, trimmed and finely sliced (preferably using a mandoline), fronds reserved
1 baby cos lettuce, roughly chopped
2 spring onions, white and green parts finely sliced
1 celery stick, chopped
100 g pomegranate seeds (see Tip)
200 g haloumi, cut into thick slices
extra-virgin olive oil, for brushing

DRESSING
3 tablespoons extra-virgin olive oil
1 tablespoon lemon juice
pinch of sea salt flakes

Combine the fennel, lettuce, spring onion, celery and pomegranate seeds in a bowl.

To make the dressing, whisk the ingredients together in a small bowl.

Brush the haloumi slices with olive oil. Heat a frying pan over medium heat, add the haloumi and pan-fry for 1 minute each side or until golden. Add to the salad bowl.

Drizzle the dressing over the salad, toss to combine, then transfer to a serving dish and serve while the haloumi is still warm.

TIP
- The easiest way to remove pomegranate seeds is to cut the fruit in half and hold one half face down in your hand with your fingers spread apart. Place a bowl under the pomegranate and bash the top of the fruit with a rolling pin to release the seeds.

Simple Lahanosalata
(GREEK CABBAGE SALAD)

SERVES 6   GF, LC, V

Easy, peasy with a little lemon squeezy! Lahanosalata is a simple low-carb salad that works perfectly alongside grilled proteins or tossed with canned tuna. Cabbage is high in vitamins C and K, folate and fibre and contains powerful antioxidants, so it's a great veggie to power you through the day. Shredded cabbage salad is perfect for a healthy lunch on the run because it maintains its texture – just pack the salad and dressing in separate containers, then dress the salad just before you're ready to eat.

½ white cabbage, finely shredded
handful of flat-leaf parsley leaves, chopped
handful of mint leaves, chopped
80 g kefalograviera cheese, shaved (see Tip)
160 g (1 cup) peas (fresh or thawed frozen)

DRESSING
3 tablespoons extra-virgin olive oil
1 tablespoon lemon juice
pinch of sea salt flakes

Combine the cabbage, fresh herbs, cheese and peas in a salad bowl.

To make the dressing, whisk the ingredients in a small bowl.

Drizzle the dressing over the salad, toss to combine and serve.

TIP
- For a dairy-free salad simply omit the cheese.

Quinoa & Herb Salad
ON A HONEY–YOGHURT BLANKET

SERVES 8   GF, V

This gorgeous salad works as a complete meal because you have protein and fibre from fluffy quinoa, vibrant green herbs and shredded cabbage all sitting prettily on a honey–yoghurt blanket. Quinoa is a complete protein, providing all nine essential amino acids, so this salad will keep you feeling fuller for longer. Quinoa is actually a seed and is commonly referred to as a 'pseudograin'. It is more closely related to spinach and beetroot than grains so it's a nutritious and filling option for those on a grain-free diet.

200 g (1 cup) white quinoa, rinsed (see Tip)
150 g (2 cups) finely shredded red cabbage
handful of coriander leaves, chopped
handful of flat-leaf parsley leaves, chopped
1 small red onion, finely sliced
75 g (½ cup) currants
2 tablespoons toasted pumpkin seeds
2 tablespoons toasted pine nuts
375 g (1½ cups) Greek yoghurt
2 tablespoons raw honey

DRESSING
80 ml (⅓ cup) extra-virgin olive oil
juice of 1 lemon
1 teaspoon dijon mustard
pinch of sea salt flakes and freshly ground
    black pepper

Place the quinoa in a saucepan with 500 ml (2 cups) of water and bring to a simmer. Cover and simmer over low heat for 10 minutes. Remove from the heat and set aside to cool with the lid on.

Combine the cooled quinoa, cabbage, fresh herbs, onion, currants and seeds in a bowl.

To make the dressing, whisk the ingredients in a bowl. Toss through the salad.

Whisk together the yoghurt and honey, then spread it over a platter. Top with the salad and serve.

TIPS
- Always rinse quinoa thoroughly before cooking to remove the bitter external coating of saponin that is naturally present to repel insects. If you skip this step your quinoa will taste bitter.

- For a dairy-free version simply substitute the Greek yoghurt for coconut yoghurt.

Charred Broccoli, Pistachio & BOCCONCINI SALAD

SERVES 6   GF, LC, V

Most people don't associate broccoli with salad but treated properly its natural firmness adds a beautiful crunch. Forget the soggy, overcooked broccoli you ate as a kid, my charred version is texturally exciting and will have you hitting your daily vitamin C and fibre requirements in no time. Broccoli pairs beautifully with most cheeses. This recipe features delicate bocconcini but you could also use a sharp cheddar or dollops of creamy ricotta.

2 tablespoons extra-virgin olive oil, plus extra for drizzling
1 garlic clove, finely sliced
½ long red chilli, deseeded and finely sliced (see Tip)
2 small heads of broccoli, cut into 2 cm pieces
45 g (⅓ cup) pistachios, roughly chopped
pinch of sea salt flakes and freshly ground black pepper
juice of 1 lemon
100 g cherry bocconcini, torn
handful of flat-leaf parsley leaves
lemon wedges, to serve

Heat the olive oil in a large frying pan or wok over low heat. Add the garlic and chilli and cook, stirring, for 30 seconds or until fragrant.

Increase the heat to medium, add the broccoli, pistachios, salt and pepper and cook for 2–3 minutes until the broccoli is tender but still reasonably firm. Squeeze in the lemon juice and toss to combine.

Transfer the broccoli mixture to a serving bowl. Scatter over the bocconcini and parsley, drizzle over a little extra olive oil and serve with lemon wedges.

TIP

- I have used half a chilli to keep the salad family friendly but you can use a whole chilli if you prefer a little more heat.

Vibrant
FATTOUSH SALAD

SERVES 8–10   DF, GF, LC, VG

This refreshing Lebanese salad is usually served with fried pieces of flatbread but I've given it a gluten-free makeover by omitting the bread and using extra capsicum, radish and pomegranate for textural crunch. The result is low carb, fresh and vibrant, with vegetables from every colour of the rainbow for maximum micronutrients. Eat the rainbow!

1 small cos lettuce, shredded
20 cherry tomatoes, halved
1 Lebanese cucumber, diced
1 small yellow capsicum, deseeded
    and finely sliced
1 small red onion, finely sliced
4 radishes, finely sliced
handful of flat-leaf parsley leaves,
    finely chopped
small handful of mint leaves, finely chopped
seeds from 1 pomegranate (see Tip, page 48)
3 teaspoons za'atar (see Tip)
2 teaspoons sumac

DRESSING
80 ml (⅓ cup) extra-virgin olive oil
juice of 1 lemon
1 small garlic clove, finely grated
1 teaspoon sea salt flakes

Combine the salad vegetables, herbs, pomegranate seeds, za'atar and sumac in a large salad bowl.

To make the dressing, whisk all the ingredients in a small bowl.

Pour the dressing over the salad, gently toss together and serve.

TIP
- Za'atar is readily available at most supermarkets, or you can make your own by blending toasted sesame seeds, sumac, dried oregano and sea salt flakes.

Greek Horiatiki Salad

SERVES 4–6   GF, LC, V

Horiatiki translates as 'village' or 'peasant' salad and it is the most famous of all Greek salads. Its popularity lies in its refreshing simplicity and relies heavily on the freshness of the produce – juicy vine-ripened tomatoes and creamy white Greek feta are a must. In most Greek tavernas the oil and vinegar are added at the table but I find it easier just to toss everything together in a bowl and top with a big block of feta for my guests to crumble.

4 vine-ripened tomatoes, cut into chunks
2 Lebanese cucumbers, halved lengthways and cut into thick slices
1 small red onion, finely sliced
1 small green or red capsicum, deseeded and finely sliced
24 whole kalamata olives
3 tablespoons extra-virgin olive oil, plus extra for drizzling
2 tablespoons red wine vinegar
pinch of sea salt flakes
200 g block of Greek feta (see Note)
good pinch of dried oregano

Combine the tomato, cucumber, onion, capsicum and olives in a salad bowl. Add the olive oil, vinegar and salt and toss to combine.

Top with the block of feta and finish with a sprinkling of oregano and an extra drizzle of olive oil.

NOTE

- Feta is a protected designation of origin (PDO) cheese, meaning it must originate from Greece. Authentic Greek feta is well worth seeking out for its superior flavour and creamy texture. Avoid 'feta-style' imitations as they are not the same.

Asian Slaw
WITH SMOKED TROUT & LIME–TAMARI DRESSING

SERVES 2–4 DF, GF, LC

When I'm eating lean and clean this is one of my go-to salads for lunch. It ticks all the boxes: low carb, high protein, nutrient dense, quick and yummy. Not only is trout high in omega 3 and rich in vitamins and minerals, it's also one of the cleanest fish you can eat because of its low mercury content. Smoked trout will keep unopened in the fridge for about a month so it's a great way to jazz up a midweek salad. Don't be afraid to use extra-virgin olive oil in Asian salads – its fruity flavour pairs beautifully with the umami notes from the tamari.

400 g whole smoked ocean or rainbow trout, deboned and flaked
75 g (1 cup) shredded green cabbage
1 baby cos lettuce, shredded
1 small carrot, julienned
2 spring onions, white and green parts finely sliced
small handful of coriander leaves, roughly chopped
2 teaspoons toasted sesame seeds

LIME–TAMARI DRESSING
2 tablespoons extra-virgin olive oil
juice of 1 lime
1 teaspoon gluten-free tamari or coconut aminos

Combine the smoked trout, cabbage, cos, carrot, spring onion, coriander and sesame seeds in a bowl.

To make the dressing, whisk the ingredients in a small bowl.

Pour the dressing over the salad, gently toss to combine and serve.

TIP
- You can replace the trout with other healthy proteins, such as tuna, smoked salmon or poached chicken.

Charred Corn
& BUCKWHEAT SALSA SALAD

SERVES 6–8 DF, GF, VG

Nourishing buckwheat bulks up this colourful protein-packed salsa, making it a filling stand-alone meal or refreshing summer side salad. Chargrilling the corn gives a smoky sweetness that contrasts beautifully with the creamy avocado, crunchy capsicum, vibrant greens and zesty lime juice. For extra heat just throw in a sliced jalapeno pepper. It's a Mexican party in a bowl!

135 g (¾ cup) raw buckwheat kernels, rinsed (see Note)
4 corn cobs, silks and husks removed
2 tablespoons extra-virgin olive oil
sea salt flakes
1 red capsicum, deseeded and diced
handful of coriander leaves, finely chopped
handful of flat-leaf parsley leaves, finely chopped
1 large avocado, diced

DRESSING
3 tablespoons extra-virgin olive oil
juice of 2 limes, plus lime halves to serve
sea salt flakes and freshly ground black pepper

Rinse the buckwheat under cold running water, then place in a small saucepan and fill with water. Boil for 8 minutes or until tender, then drain, rinse and set aside to cool to room temperature.

Brush the corn with the olive oil and sprinkle with salt. Heat a chargrill pan over high heat, add the corn and cook, turning regularly, for 15 minutes or until tender and nicely charred all over. Cool slightly, then slice off the kernels.

Combine the buckwheat, corn kernels, capsicum, fresh herbs and avocado in a salad bowl.

To make the dressing, whisk the ingredients in a small bowl.

Drizzle the dressing over the salad, gently toss to combine and serve with lime halves on the side.

NOTE
- Buckwheat is a nutritious seed which, despite its name, does not contain any wheat. It is considered a superfood because it is high in protein, fibre, antioxidants and minerals.

Sizzling Vietnamese
BEEF NOODLE SALAD BOWLS

SERVES 4 DF, GF

A tangle of rice noodles creates the perfect nest for crunchy veggies, fresh herbs and sizzling eye fillet in these mouthwatering Vietnamese salad bowls. The most common condiment in Vietnamese cooking is fish sauce (rather than soy) so most Vietnamese dishes naturally sit in the gluten-free space. Eye fillet is my preferred cut of steak when stir-frying because it is unbelievably tender and soaks up the marinade and dressing beautifully.

2 tablespoons gluten-free tamari or coconut aminos
1 tablespoon gluten-free oyster sauce
2 garlic cloves, finely grated
1 teaspoon sesame oil
400 g beef eye fillet, very finely sliced
2 tablespoons peanut oil
3 tablespoons roasted salted peanuts, chopped
1 tablespoon Asian fried shallots (see Tips)

DRESSING
2 tablespoons fish sauce
1 tablespoon rice vinegar
2 teaspoons caster sugar
juice of 1 lime, plus lime wedges to serve

SALAD
250 g rice vermicelli noodles
1 large Lebanese cucumber, halved, deseeded and sliced diagonally
1 large carrot, julienned
handful of coriander leaves
small handful of Vietnamese mint leaves

Combine the tamari or coconut aminos, oyster sauce, garlic and sesame oil in a bowl. Add the beef and stir to coat, then cover and marinate for at least 30 minutes (or overnight in the fridge if time permits).

To make the dressing, whisk the ingredients in a small bowl.

To prepare the salad, cook the noodles according to the packet instructions and set aside to cool, then divide among four bowls. Top with the cucumber, carrot, coriander and mint.

Heat a little peanut oil in a large wok over high heat. Working in batches, add the beef and stir-fry for 1 minute each side or until caramelised, adding more oil as needed. Take care not to overcrowd the wok or the meat will stew.

Add the beef to the salad bowls and pour over the dressing. Garnish with the peanuts and fried shallots and serve with lime wedges on the side.

TIPS

- Asian fried shallots are readily available at Asian grocery stores or in the Asian aisle of larger supermarkets. Alternatively you can make your own by frying a finely sliced Asian shallot in olive oil over low heat for 2–3 minutes until golden, then draining on paper towel.

- For a low-carb version simply omit the rice noodles and add extra veggies.

- You can replace the eye fillet with chicken, prawns or pork.

Maple-roasted Sweet Potato,
BABY SPINACH & CANDIED PECAN SALAD

SERVES 6   DF, GF, VG

Sweet potato, maple syrup, cinnamon and pecans roasting away together. You can already taste it, right? All the magic happens in the oven so the only tasks that remain are to scatter greens on a platter and make the dressing. Roasting enhances the natural sweetness of potato, resulting in a crisp caramelised exterior and a soft mushy centre. You can swap the sweet potato for pumpkin if you like – it's just as delicious.

1 large sweet potato, peeled and cut
  into wedges
2 tablespoons extra-virgin olive oil
2 tablespoons pure maple syrup
½ teaspoon ground cinnamon
pinch of sea salt flakes and freshly ground
  black pepper
50 g (½ cup) pecans, roughly chopped
2 large handfuls of baby spinach leaves
2 large handfuls of rocket leaves

DRESSING
3 tablespoons extra-virgin olive oil
1 tablespoon balsamic vinegar
1 small garlic clove, finely grated
sea salt flakes and freshly ground black pepper

Preheat the oven to 200°C (fan-forced) and line a baking tray with baking paper.

Combine the sweet potato, olive oil, maple syrup, cinnamon, salt and pepper in a bowl and toss to combine. Transfer to the prepared tray and roast for 15 minutes or until the potato is cooked through. Remove the tray from the oven, add the pecans and gently toss through. Return to the oven and roast for another 15 minutes. Remove and allow to cool for 2–3 minutes.

Meanwhile, to make the dressing, whisk all the ingredients in a small bowl.

Arrange the spinach and rocket leaves on a serving platter. Top with the warm sweet potato mixture, drizzle over the dressing and serve.

TIP
- If you love your sweet potatoes and pecans even more caramelised just add another 1–2 tablespoons of pure maple syrup prior to roasting.

Crispy Wedge Salad
WITH GREEN GODDESS DRESSING

SERVES 6   GF, LC

Green goddess is a classic Californian dressing that can transform simple lettuce into something truly magical. Imagine a cold crispy wedge of lettuce blanketed in a creamy, herby dressing topped with salty bacon and crunchy snow peas. Yum! Wedge salads look dramatic when they hit the table but they definitely tick the 'quick and super easy' box.

4 bacon rashers, fat trimmed, diced
1 iceberg lettuce, cut into 6 wedges
150 g snow peas, trimmed and sliced in half lengthways
3 tablespoons finely chopped chives

GREEN GODDESS DRESSING
3 tablespoons Greek yoghurt (or coconut yoghurt for a dairy-free version)
½ avocado
1 garlic clove, bashed
2 anchovy fillets, chopped
small handful of flat-leaf parsley leaves
10 basil leaves
juice of 1 lemon
1 teaspoon sea salt flakes
2 tablespoons extra-virgin olive oil

To make the green goddess dressing, place the ingredients in a food processor and blitz until smooth.

Place the bacon in a cold frying pan and cook over low heat until the fat has rendered out. Increase the heat to medium and cook the bacon until crisp. Remove and drain on paper towel.

Arrange the lettuce wedges in a line on a rectangular serving platter. Drizzle the dressing over the top, scatter with the bacon, snow peas and chives, and serve.

TIP
- You can make the dressing in advance and store it in the fridge for up to 3 days.

Watermelon, Feta
& BLACK SESAME SALAD

SERVES 6–8   GF, LC, V

This refreshing summer salad is inspired by my childhood love of ice-cold watermelon topped with salty feta – a classic Greek pairing. Zesty lime juice enhances the sweetness of the watermelon, mint and cucumber both add freshness, and black sesame seeds give a welcome nuttiness and interesting textural finish. A simple salad that packs a big flavour punch!

1 kg chilled watermelon, rind removed,
   cut into wedges
1 large Lebanese cucumber, sliced diagonally
100 g Greek feta, cut into cubes
handful of mint leaves, finely shredded, small
   leaves left whole
1 tablespoon black sesame seeds

DRESSING
3 tablespoons extra-virgin olive oil
juice of 1 large or 2 small limes
pinch of sea salt flakes and freshly ground
   black pepper

Arrange the watermelon wedges on a serving platter. Top with the cucumber and feta.

To make the dressing, whisk the ingredients in a small bowl.

Drizzle the dressing over the salad, scatter with the mint and sesame seeds, and serve.

TIP
- If you are entertaining you can prep the watermelon wedges and cucumber ahead of time and arrange on a platter, then top with the remaining ingredients just before serving to maintain freshness.

Tropical Prawn, Mango
& BUTTER LETTUCE SALAD

SERVES 6   DF, GF, LC

Nothing screams summer like ripe, juicy mangoes and succulent prawns. Throw in aromatic herbs, creamy avocado and a zesty lime dressing drizzled into crisp lettuce cups and you are in summer salad heaven. Avocado oil has sublime buttery notes and is high in oleic acid, antioxidants and vitamin E. If you don't have avocado oil, olive oil also works well and is just as healthy.

24 cooked king prawns, peeled and deveined,
   tails intact
1 large Calypso mango, cut into cubes (see Tip)
1 large avocado, cut into cubes
small handful of coriander leaves, finely
   chopped, plus extra leaves to serve
small handful of Vietnamese mint leaves,
   finely chopped
1 butter lettuce, leaves separated
3 tablespoons salted roasted cashews, chopped

DRESSING
3 tablespoons avocado or extra-virgin olive oil
juice of 1 large lime
1 teaspoon finely grated ginger
pinch of sea salt flakes and freshly ground
   black pepper

Combine the prawns, mango, avocado, coriander and mint in a bowl.

To make the dressing, whisk the ingredients in a small bowl.

Drizzle the dressing over the salad and gently toss to combine.

Arrange butter lettuce leaves on a platter and spoon the salad on top. Drizzle over any remaining dressing and sprinkle with the cashews and extra coriander.

TIP
- I prefer to use Calypso mangoes because they have firmer flesh and a tangier flavour than other varieties, but any mango will do. If mangoes are not in season you can replace them with tropical papaya, which is available all year round.

Roasted Cauliflower, CHICKPEA & ALMOND SALAD

SERVES 8 DF, GF, VG

Cauliflower is one of the hardest-working veggies around – it can be roasted, boiled, pureed, fried, seared or eaten raw, plus it's a great carrier of other flavours. This robust winter salad is boosted with fibre and protein from nourishing chickpeas and crunchy almonds. The herbs add freshness and you get the perfect acidic punch from the red wine vinaigrette.

1 head of cauliflower, cut into florets
400 g can chickpeas, drained and rinsed
2 tablespoons extra-virgin olive oil
pinch of sea salt flakes and freshly ground
   black pepper
handful of flat-leaf parsley leaves, chopped
small handful of mint leaves, chopped
3 tablespoons slivered almonds, toasted

VINAIGRETTE
3 tablespoons extra-virgin olive oil
1 tablespoon red wine vinegar
1 golden shallot, finely diced
1 teaspoon dijon mustard
pinch of sea salt flakes and freshly ground
   black pepper

Preheat the oven to 200°C (fan-forced) and line a baking tray with baking paper.

Place the cauliflower and chickpeas on the prepared tray, add the olive oil and salt and pepper, and toss to coat. Spread out in a single layer and roast for 30 minutes or until golden, tossing occasionally to ensure even browning. Remove and cool for a few minutes.

Transfer the warm cauliflower and chickpeas to a serving bowl and add the fresh herbs and almonds.

To make the dressing, whisk the ingredients in a small bowl.

Drizzle the dressing over the salad and toss to combine. Serve.

NOTE
- Cauliflower is considered a superfood because it is high in fibre, protein, antioxidants and vitamins B and C.

SOUPS

Creamy Celeriac & Apple Soup
(WITHOUT CREAM!)

SERVES 4–6   DF, GF, VG

Place this bowl of silky goodness in front of anyone and I guarantee they'll assume it is loaded with cream. But they'd be wrong! Celeriac and celery are part of the same family but celeriac has an earthier flavour and starchier texture so it purees beautifully in soups. The tart apple adds a very subtle sweetness and potato boosts the creaminess ... without the cream!

3 tablespoons extra-virgin olive oil,
  plus extra to serve
1 onion, chopped
1 celeriac, peeled and cut into 2 cm cubes
1 tablespoon sea salt flakes
1 garlic clove, chopped
2 teaspoons thyme leaves, plus extra to serve
1 floury potato, peeled and cut into 2 cm cubes
1 large granny smith apple, peeled, cored
  and roughly chopped, plus extra, julienned,
  to serve
750 ml (3 cups) gluten-free vegetable stock
freshly ground black pepper

Heat the olive oil in a large saucepan over medium heat, add the onion, celeriac and salt and sauté for 5 minutes to soften the vegetables. Add the garlic and thyme and sauté for another 30 seconds.

Add the potato, apple and stock. Reduce the heat to low and simmer, covered, for 20 minutes or until the vegetables are nice and soft. Using a hand-held blender or food processor, blitz the soup to a smooth puree.

Ladle the soup into bowls and season with a good grinding of pepper. Garnish with extra apple and thyme and finish with an extra drizzle of olive oil.

NOTE

- Celeriac is a nutrition powerhouse packed with antioxidants, fibre, vitamins B6, C and K and important minerals.

Vasili's Chicken
AVGOLEMONO SOUP

SERVES 4–6 DF, GF

My son Vasili loves a comforting bowl of creamy Greek chicken soup with avgolemono, a lemon–egg sauce, particularly during the cold and flu season. This classic soup has a neutral stock, meaning it is only seasoned with the best-quality sea salt flakes for a pure chicken flavour. Once I attempted to sneak in celery and a few bay leaves but Vasili would not have it; he made it very clear he did not want me messing with Yiayia's village recipe!

1 x 1.5 kg chicken
sea salt flakes and freshly ground black pepper
200 g (1 cup) medium-grain rice
2 eggs, at room temperature (see Tips)
juice of 2 lemons, plus extra if needed

Place the chicken in a medium saucepan and pour in 2 litres of cold water. Add a very generous pinch of salt and bring to a simmer. Cover and simmer gently over low heat for 1 hour.

Once cooked, remove the chicken from the pan and set aside to cool slightly. When the chicken is cool enough to handle, remove and discard the skin, and shred the meat.

Strain the stock into a smaller saucepan. Add the rice to the strained stock. Bring to the boil, then reduce the heat and simmer for 12 minutes or until the rice is al dente. Remove from the heat (it will keep cooking in the residual heat so you don't want it too soft).

Whisk the eggs in a bowl, then pour in the lemon juice and whisk to combine. Very slowly whisk in 250 ml (1 cup) of the warm chicken stock until the mixture is creamy, then pour it back into the stock and gently stir to combine. Taste and adjust the seasoning with more salt or lemon juice if needed.

Divide most of the shredded chicken among bowls and pour over the hot soup. Finish with a grinding of pepper and the remaining shredded chicken.

TIPS

- It's important that the eggs are at room temperature, otherwise they will curdle when whisked with the chicken stock.

- Add the lemon juice just before whisking in the warm stock so the acid does not cook the eggs while they are sitting.

Hearty Chicken Drumstick
& VEGETABLE SOUP

SERVES 4–6   DF, GF, LC

On a chilly winter's day there is nothing I love more than a hearty bowl of chicken soup loaded with healthy veggies, ginger and garlic to boost my immunity. Crammed with superfood goodness from pumpkin and silverbeet and protein from lean chicken, this soup is low carb, bursting with antioxidants and insanely delicious. The silverbeet reduces quite a bit in the pan so don't be concerned if it looks like you have chopped too much.

6 chicken drumsticks
sea salt flakes
3 tablespoons extra-virgin olive oil
1 large onion, chopped
1 large carrot, halved and sliced
1 celery stalk, sliced
2 garlic cloves, finely grated
1 tablespoon finely grated ginger
200 g silverbeet, chopped
220 g peeled butternut pumpkin,
   cut into 3 cm cubes
juice of 1 lemon
freshly ground black pepper

Generously season the chicken drumsticks with salt. Heat 2 tablespoons of olive oil in a wide-based saucepan over medium heat. Sear the drumsticks for about 5 minutes, turning to colour on all sides, then remove from the pan and set aside.

Heat the remaining olive oil in the pan, add the onion, carrot, celery and a pinch of salt and sauté for 5 minutes or until softened. Add the garlic and ginger and sauté for another 30 seconds.

Return the drumsticks to the pan and pour in 2 litres of water. Cover and simmer over low heat for 45 minutes.

Add the silverbeet and pumpkin and simmer, covered, for another 10–15 minutes until the vegetables are tender.

Remove the chicken drumsticks from the soup. Allow to cool a little, then peel off the skin, shred the meat and return it to the soup. Stir in the lemon juice, season with pepper and serve.

TIPS

- You can replace the silverbeet with other healthy greens, such as spinach or kale.

- Use sweet potato instead of pumpkin, if preferred.

- I use chicken drumsticks because they are cheap and easy to cook with, but you can use any cut of chicken. Make sure it is still on the bone to add more flavour.

Nourishing Fakes
(GREEK LENTIL SOUP)

SERVES 4–6   DF, GF, VG

Fakes is a traditional Greek vegan soup commonly eating during the fasting season. I regularly make it as a nourishing meat-free Monday meal when I want to eat something hearty but clean. Lentils are high in protein, fibre, iron and folate, making them an excellent gluten-free option for dinner. This soup really comes to life at the final stage when you add a splash of acidic vinegar to enhance all the flavours. It's even tastier as a packed lunch for work the next day!

250 g lentils (green or brown)
3 tablespoons extra-virgin olive oil
1 onion, finely diced
1 large carrot, finely diced
1 celery stalk, finely diced
sea salt flakes and freshly ground black pepper
2 garlic cloves, finely grated
2 dried bay leaves
1 teaspoon finely chopped rosemary leaves
400 g can crushed tomatoes
1.5 litres gluten-free vegetable stock or water
1 tablespoon red wine vinegar
gluten-free crusty bread, to serve

Rinse the lentils thoroughly, then drain and set aside.

Heat the olive oil in a saucepan over low heat. Add the onion, carrot, celery and a generous pinch of salt and sauté for 5 minutes or until softened. Add the garlic, bay leaves and rosemary and cook for another 30 seconds.

Pour in the crushed tomatoes and stock or water, add the lentils and bring to a simmer. Cover and simmer over low heat for 45 minutes or until the lentils are tender.

Remove the pan from the heat and stir in the vinegar. Season to taste with salt and pepper and serve with gluten-free crusty bread.

TIP

- In Greece this soup is traditionally served with something salty, such as feta, olives or sardines.

The Greenest Pea
& HAM SOUP

SERVES 4–6   DF, GF, LC

Hearty, sweet and bright, bright green. This is quite possibly the prettiest and easiest soup you will ever make, all thanks to a bag of frozen peas – a freezer essential for any time-poor cook. I replace traditional dried peas with frozen because they cook in a fraction of the time and result in the most glorious shade of green. It's easy peasy!

1 tablespoon extra-virgin olive oil
1 onion, finely chopped
2 garlic cloves, finely grated
1 sebago potato (or another floury variety),
   peeled and cut into 2 cm cubes
800 g frozen peas
sea salt flakes and freshly ground
   black pepper

STOCK
1.5 kg ham hock
1 small onion, halved and peeled
5 thyme sprigs
3 garlic cloves, peeled

Place the stock ingredients in a saucepan and pour in enough cold water to just cover the ham hock. Simmer, covered, over low heat for 1½ hours. Remove the ham hock and leave to cool slightly, then shred the meat. Strain the stock into a bowl, discarding the solids.

Heat the olive oil in a saucepan over medium–high heat. Add the onion and sauté for 5 minutes or until softened. Add the garlic and cook for another 30 seconds. Add the potato and 1 litre of the strained stock and simmer, covered, for 15 minutes or until the potato is tender. Stir in the frozen peas and cook for an additional 1 minute.

Take the soup off the heat and blitz with a hand-held blender or in a food processor until smooth. Taste and season if needed – the stock will already be quite salty from the ham.

Ladle the soup into bowls and garnish generously with the shredded ham.

Roasted Carrot
& CUMIN SOUP

SERVES 4–6   DF, GF, LC

The best way to maximise flavour in carrot soup is to roast the carrots first, which will caramelise their natural sugars and enhance their sweetness. To wake up the carrot I add aromatic cumin, coriander, garlic and ginger, and a swirl of creamy yoghurt at the final stage to balance out all those zesty spices. This is a simple soup with few ingredients but it has a surprisingly complex flavour.

1 kg carrots, cut into 2 cm-thick slices
2 teaspoons ground cumin
1 teaspoon ground coriander
1 tablespoon sea salt flakes
80 ml (⅓ cup) extra-virgin olive oil
1 onion, finely chopped
3 cm piece of ginger, finely grated
2 garlic cloves, finely grated
1 litre gluten-free vegetable or chicken stock

TO SERVE
dollop of Greek or coconut yoghurt
flat-leaf parsley sprigs
freshly ground black pepper

Preheat the oven to 200°C (fan-forced) and line a baking tray with baking paper.

Place the carrot on the prepared tray, add the cumin, coriander, salt and 3 tablespoons of the olive oil and toss to coat well. Roast for 40 minutes or until the carrot is tender, tossing occasionally for even browning.

Heat the remaining olive oil in a saucepan over low heat, add the onion and sauté for 5 minutes or until softened. Add the ginger and garlic and sauté for another 30 seconds. Add the roasted carrot and pour in the stock, then simmer gently for 5 minutes.

Take the soup off the heat and blitz with a hand-held blender or in a food processor until smooth.

Ladle the soup into bowls and swirl through a dollop of yoghurt. Finish with a little parsley and a good grinding of pepper.

NOTES

Carrots are a fantastic source of fibre, beta-carotene, vitamin K and antioxidants.

To make this soup vegan, use vegetable stock and top with coconut yoghurt.

Thai Sweet Potato Soup
WITH ROASTED CASHEWS

SERVES 4–6   DF, GF, VG

Sweet potato is beautiful in soups because it has a thick, creamy texture when pureed and carries other flavours well, particularly spices that balance its natural sweetness. If you love extra heat feel free to increase the quantity of curry paste in this recipe; I keep mine fairly mild so it's family friendly.

1 tablespoon coconut oil
1 onion, finely chopped
1 tablespoon finely grated ginger
2 garlic cloves, finely grated
2 tablespoons gluten-free Thai red curry paste
1 kg sweet potatoes, peeled and cut into
   3 cm cubes
1 tablespoon gluten-free tamari or
   coconut aminos
750 ml (3 cups) gluten-free vegetable stock
125 ml (½ cup) coconut milk
juice of 1 lime
sea salt flakes and freshly ground black pepper
handful of chopped roasted cashews, to serve
handful of coriander leaves, to serve

Melt the coconut oil in a large saucepan over medium heat, add the onion and sauté for 5 minutes or until softened. Add the ginger, garlic and curry paste and sauté for another 2 minutes.

Add the sweet potato, tamari or coconut aminos and stock. Reduce the heat to low and simmer, covered, for 20 minutes or until the potato has softened.

Take the soup off the heat and stir in the coconut milk and lime juice. Blitz with a hand-held blender or in a food processor until smooth and creamy. Adjust the seasoning to taste.

Ladle the soup into bowls and top with cashews and coriander.

NOTE

- Sweet potatoes are a great source of fibre, vitamins and beta-carotene, a powerful antioxidant that gives orange fruits and vegetables their colour.

Velvety Cauliflower Soup
WITH HAZELNUT DUKKAH

SERVES 4–6 DF, GF, LC, VG

This soup is so velvety and creamy, your family and friends will be surprised to discover it is completely dairy free and low carb. Pureed cauliflower has a beautiful silky texture and the addition of coconut cream with a sprinkling of dukkah makes this soup dreamy and creamy! Dukkah is an Egyptian spice blend consisting of nuts and seeds and it is super easy to make at home. I love homemade dukkah sprinkled over soups, veggies and smashed avocado toast for breakfast.

2 tablespoons extra-virgin olive oil
1 large onion, finely chopped
2 garlic cloves, finely grated
1 tablespoon thyme leaves
1 head of cauliflower (about 800 g),
    cut into florets
500 ml (2 cups) gluten-free vegetable stock
125 ml (½ cup) coconut cream
pinch of sea salt flakes and freshly ground
    black pepper
chopped chives, to serve

HAZELNUT DUKKAH
70 g (½ cup) blanched hazelnuts
3 tablespoons sesame seeds
1 tablespoon coriander seeds
1 tablespoon cumin seeds
1 teaspoon sea salt flakes

Heat the olive oil in a large saucepan over medium heat, add the onion and sauté for 5 minutes or until softened. Add the garlic and thyme and cook for 30 seconds.

Add the cauliflower, stock, coconut cream, salt and pepper, then reduce the heat to low and simmer for 20 minutes. Blitz with a hand-held blender or in a food processor until smooth and creamy.

Meanwhile, to make the dukkah, toast the hazelnuts in a large dry frying pan over low heat for 2–3 minutes until slightly coloured. Add the sesame, coriander and cumin seeds and toast for 2–3 minutes until golden and fragrant. Add the salt, transfer the mixture to a mortar and pestle or food processor and lightly crush. Don't make it too fine – you still want a bit of texture.

Ladle the soup into bowls and serve with a sprinkling of hazelnut dukkah and chives.

TIPS

- Store your homemade dukkah in an airtight container for up to 4 weeks. Change things up a bit each time you make a new batch – almonds, pistachios and pine nuts are all good.

- If you are not following a vegetarian diet you can replace the vegetable stock with gluten-free chicken stock for added depth of flavour.

Psarosoupa
(FISH SOUP)

SERVES 4–6   DF, GF

When I was a kid psarosoupa was not something I enjoyed eating, but as an adult I can't get enough of the delicate chunks of snapper and hearty vegetables floating in a delicious fish broth. Snapper is my favourite but you can replace it with any firm white fish, such as cod or mullet. It is important to simmer the fish with the skin and bones intact to maximise the flavour of your stock.

1 whole snapper (about 1.2 kg), cleaned
   and cut into 3 pieces
2 dried bay leaves
10 black peppercorns
sea salt flakes
3 tablespoons extra-virgin olive oil
1 onion, diced
1 large carrot, halved and sliced diagonally
1 large celery stalk, sliced diagonally,
   a few leaves reserved to serve
2 sebago potatoes (or another floury variety),
   peeled and cut into 3 cm cubes
juice of 1 lemon, plus extra if needed
freshly ground black pepper
handful of flat-leaf parsley leaves

Place the fish in a large saucepan and add the bay leaves, peppercorns, 3 teaspoons of salt and 2 litres of water. Cover and simmer over low heat for 30 minutes. Remove the fish from the pan and strain the murky fish stock into a bowl, discarding the solids.

Heat the olive oil in a medium saucepan over low heat, add the onion, carrot, celery, potato and a pinch of salt and sauté for 5 minutes or until the vegetables start to soften. Pour in the fish stock and simmer, covered, for 20 minutes or until the vegetables are nice and tender.

Remove the fish meat from the bones, discard the bones and skin and add the fish to the stock, along with the lemon juice. Taste and add more salt or lemon juice if necessary.

Ladle the soup into bowls and season with pepper. Top with parsley and celery leaves and serve.

TIP
- For a more intense flavour, ask your fishmonger for extra fish heads and bones (anything but salmon, which is too overpowering) to add to the pan when preparing the stock.

Youverlakia
(MEATBALL, LEMON & DILL SOUP)

SERVES 4–6   DF, GF

'Meatballs' suggests this Greek soup will be heavy but I promise it is anything but. The mince is rolled with rice and fresh herbs, keeping the meatballs light and airy, and the stock is zesty thanks to the avgolemono (lemon–egg) sauce. The result is a light and playful soup with fluffy meatballs floating in it – perfect for little ones.

2 tablespoons extra-virgin olive oil
2 dried bay leaves
sea salt flakes and freshly ground black pepper
finely chopped flat-leaf parsley leaves, to serve

MEATBALLS
500 g beef mince
100 g (½ cup) medium-grain rice
1 large onion, grated, excess moisture
    squeezed out
1 garlic clove, finely grated
1 egg
3 tablespoons finely chopped dill fronds
3 tablespoons finely chopped flat-leaf
    parsley leaves
1 tablespoon sea salt flakes
pinch of ground white pepper

AVGOLEMONO (LEMON–EGG SAUCE)
2 eggs, at room temperature
juice of 1 large lemon, plus extra if needed

To make the meatballs, place the ingredients in a bowl and mix well with your hands. Pop in the fridge for 30 minutes to firm up, then roll the mixture into 20 small meatballs and set aside.

Combine the olive oil, bay leaves, a pinch of salt and 1.5 litres of water in a saucepan. Bring to a gentle boil, then slowly add the meatballs. Simmer over low heat for 20 minutes or until the meatballs are cooked through, skimming the surface occasionally to remove any scum. Take off the heat.

To make the avgolemono, whisk the eggs in a medium bowl, then pour in the lemon juice and whisk to combine. Very slowly whisk in a few ladlefuls of the warm soup until the mixture is creamy, then pour it back into the soup and gently stir to combine. Taste and adjust the seasoning with more salt or lemon juice if needed.

Divide the meatballs and soup among bowls, sprinkle with parsley and finish with a good grinding of pepper.

VEGETABLES

Balsamic & Honey-glazed
CARROTS WITH HAZELNUTS

SERVES 4–6   DF, GF, LC, V

Beautifully glazed and sticky on the outside, soft and tender on the inside, these carrots are a showstopper. The sprinkling of crushed hazelnuts adds an interesting textural element, elevating the humble carrot to another level. Ensure that you leave a short stub of leafy greens intact for a beautiful rustic presentation.

500 g dutch carrots, peeled and trimmed
2 tablespoons extra-virgin olive oil
2 tablespoons balsamic vinegar
1 tablespoon raw honey
1 teaspoon sea salt flakes
pinch of freshly ground black pepper
40 g (⅓ cup) chopped hazelnuts

Preheat the oven to 200°C (fan-forced) and line a baking tray with baking paper.

Place the carrots on the prepared tray, add the olive oil, vinegar, honey, salt and pepper and toss to combine.

Roast for 30 minutes, tossing halfway through cooking for even browning. Transfer to a serving plate, top with the hazelnuts and serve.

Gigantes
(BAKED LIMA BEANS IN TOMATO & VEGETABLE SAUCE)

SERVES 8–10   DF, GF, VG

This nourishing vegan meal made with 'giant beans' is commonly shared during Lent in Greece when people want to cook super-comforting and filling food. It's totally delicious as is, though for a non-vegan version you can ramp it up by crumbling feta over the hot beans as I've done here. Make sure you have some crusty gluten-free bread on hand to mop up the beautiful sauce.

300 g dried butter beans (also known as lima beans)
80 ml (⅓ cup) extra-virgin olive oil, plus extra for drizzling
1 large onion, diced
1 large carrot, diced
1 celery stalk, cut into 1 cm-thick slices
1 small red capsicum, deseeded and chopped
sea salt flakes and freshly ground black pepper
2 garlic cloves, finely grated
2 dried bay leaves
1 cinnamon stick
1 teaspoon sweet paprika
2 tablespoons tomato paste
2 tablespoons sherry vinegar
400 g can crushed tomatoes
375 ml (1½ cups) gluten-free vegetable stock or water
100 g Greek feta, crumbled (optional)
small handful of chopped flat-leaf parsley leaves

Soak the beans in a bowl of water overnight. Drain and rinse, then place in a large saucepan and fill with cold water. Simmer the beans over low heat for 20 minutes or until just tender, skimming off any peeled skins or scum that float to the surface. Drain, then transfer to a rectangular baking dish (about 30 cm × 25 cm).

Preheat the oven to 180°C (fan-forced).

Heat the olive oil in the same saucepan over medium heat. Add the onion, carrot, celery, capsicum and a generous pinch of salt and sauté for 10 minutes or until softened. Add the garlic, bay leaves, cinnamon, paprika and tomato paste and cook for another 30 seconds. Pour in the sherry vinegar, stirring to release any caramelised bits caught on the base of the pan, and simmer for 30 seconds or until reduced slightly.

Add the crushed tomatoes and stock or water and bring to a simmer. Taste and season with salt and pepper if necessary, then pour over the beans and stir to combine.

Cover the dish tightly with baking paper then foil and bake for 45 minutes. Remove the paper and foil, then bake for a further 15 minutes.

Remove the dish from the oven. Scatter over the feta (if using) and parsley, drizzle with extra olive oil and serve.

Broccolini with
WARM SESAME-CRUSTED FETA
DRIZZLED WITH HONEY

SERVES 4–6   GF, LC, V

My mother comes from the beautiful Greek island of Crete, the birthplace of sesame-crusted feta drizzled with honey. Traditionally, the feta is fried, but in this recipe I bake it in the oven with broccolini for a stunning vegetarian dish crammed with contrasting flavours and textures. It's salty, sweet, creamy, crispy and, most importantly, super easy because it's all baked on one tray.

40 g (⅓ cup) tapioca flour
freshly ground black pepper
1 egg, lightly whisked
80 g (½ cup) sesame seeds
200 g Greek feta, cut into cubes
600 g broccolini
2 tablespoons extra-virgin olive oil
1 tablespoon balsamic vinegar
sea salt flakes
2 teaspoons raw honey

Preheat the oven to 180°C (fan-forced) and line a large baking tray with baking paper.

Set up three dipping stations: tapioca flour seasoned with pepper in one bowl, egg in another, and sesame seeds in the last.

Dust the feta cubes in the flour, shaking off the excess, then dip them in the egg and coat in the sesame seeds. Place the feta cubes on one side of the prepared tray and bake for 20 minutes.

Remove the tray from the oven. Place the broccolini in a bowl and toss with the olive oil, vinegar and a little salt and pepper. Arrange in a single layer on the other side of the tray and bake for a further 15 minutes or until the broccolini is tender and crispy and the feta is golden.

Transfer the broccolini to a platter, scatter over the warm feta cubes and drizzle with the honey.

Cauliflower Steaks
WITH SMOKY BABA GHANOUSH

SERVES 4–6   DF, GF, LC, VG

Plant-based steaks are not only delicious and filling, they provide the perfect blank canvas for myriad seasonings and dressings. I have a little shortcut to reduce the cauliflower roasting time: microwave the steaks to soften the inside before blasting them in a hot oven for 20 minutes until crisp and golden. Serve with smoky baba ghanoush for creaminess and a sprinkling of toasted almonds, juicy pomegranate seeds and fresh herbs for added pops of flavour and texture. You won't miss the red meat!

1 large head of cauliflower, stem removed, then cut into four 3 cm-thick steaks, loose florets reserved
3 tablespoons extra-virgin olive oil
pinch of sea salt flakes and freshly ground black pepper

BABA GHANOUSH

2 large eggplants
2 tablespoons extra-virgin olive oil
1 tablespoon tahini
2 garlic cloves, finely grated
juice of 1 lemon
1 teaspoon ground cumin
pinch of sea salt flakes

TO SERVE

mint leaves
finely chopped flat-leaf parsley leaves
pomegranate seeds
toasted slivered almonds

Preheat the oven to 200°C (fan-forced) and line a baking tray with baking paper.

To make the baba ghanoush, cook the eggplants directly over an open flame for 10 minutes, turning regularly until the skin is charred and blistered (see Note). Place the eggplants in a bowl, cover with plastic wrap and allow to cool. When they are cool enough to handle, peel away the skin and place the flesh in a sieve, pressing on it firmly to strain the liquid into the bowl. Discard the liquid and transfer the flesh to a food processor, add the remaining ingredients and blitz until smooth.

Meanwhile, place the cauliflower steaks and loose florets on a plate and cook in the microwave on high for 6 minutes to soften. Transfer the cauliflower to the prepared tray, drizzle with olive oil and season with salt and pepper. Massage the oil and seasoning all over the cauliflower, then roast for 20 minutes or until golden and crispy.

To serve, spoon the baba ghanoush onto a serving plate, top with the cauliflower and garnish with fresh herbs, pomegranate seeds and almonds.

NOTE

- If you do not have a gas stove, you can cook the eggplants either in a hot frying pan, turning regularly for even cooking, or roast the eggplants in a 200°C (fan-forced) oven for 30–40 minutes until the flesh is soft.

Smashed Pea & Corn Fritters
WITH LIME AVOCADO

SERVES 4–6   DF, GF, V

Peas and corn add a beautiful sweetness to these crispy fritters and the vibrant green herbs pack in freshness and bags of flavour. By smashing half the peas and corn in the first step you create a paste to bind the fritters – that's the wonderful thing about working with veggies that can be pureed, fried or baked. These fritters are perfect as a stand-alone meal for breakfast, lunch or dinner, and are delicious in wraps, burger buns and lunchboxes, too.

extra-virgin olive oil, for frying

FRITTERS
235 g (1½ cups) frozen peas
150 g (1 cup) frozen corn kernels
60 g (½ cup) tapioca flour
2 spring onions, finely sliced
small handful of mint leaves, finely chopped
small handful of coriander leaves,
    finely chopped
1 egg, whisked
1 teaspoon gluten-free baking powder
1 teaspoon ground cumin
2 teaspoons sea salt flakes
pinch of freshly ground black pepper

LIME AVOCADO
1 large ripe avocado
juice of 1 lime, plus extra lime wedges to serve
1 tablespoon finely chopped coriander leaves
pinch of sea salt and freshly ground
    black pepper

To make the fritters, blanch the peas and corn in a saucepan of salted boiling water for 2 minutes, then drain. Place half the peas and corn in a large bowl and set aside. Smash the other half with a mortar and pestle to form a chunky paste. Add the paste to the bowl, along with the remaining ingredients, and mix with your hands to combine.

To make the lime avocado, mash all the ingredients together in a bowl.

Heat a large frying pan over medium heat. Add enough olive oil to coat the base of the pan, then spoon in ¼ cup portions of batter. Cook for 3 minutes on each side until golden and crispy. Depending on the size of your pan you may need to cook them in batches, adding more oil as required.

Serve the fritters with the lime avocado and extra lime wedges.

VARIATIONS
- For a vegan version, replace the egg with 1 tablespoon of ground chia seeds mixed with 3 tablespoons of water until it goes gooey.

- If dairy isn't an issue, add 100 g of your favourite grated cheese to the fritter mixture.

Chunky Greek Oven Fries
WITH FETA

SERVES 4 GF, V

Patates with crumbled feta is a staple side at any Greek taverna. As much as I love a bowl of crispy hand-cut fries, I rarely deep-fry at home. These chunky baked fries are just as crisp and delicious, minus the fat, calories and oily mess. To keep the fries extra crisp, remember to pat the potato dry with paper towel prior to baking. Simple and quick to prepare, you'll never revert to fried chips again!

600 g sebago potatoes (or another floury variety), peeled and cut into 1.5 cm-thick chips
2 tablespoons extra-virgin olive oil
2 teaspoons sea salt flakes
1 teaspoon dried Greek oregano, plus extra sprigs to serve
100 g Greek feta

Preheat the oven to 200°C (fan-forced) and line a baking tray with baking paper.

Dry the potato with paper towel to remove excess moisture. Spread the fries evenly over the prepared tray. Drizzle with the olive oil, scatter over the sea salt and oregano and toss to coat.

Bake for 30 minutes until golden brown, tossing halfway for even cooking. Serve immediately with the feta crumbled over the top and a little extra oregano.

Rockin' Ratatouille

SERVES 8–10   DF, GF, LC, VG

This classic baked vegetable dish is usually presented in a rustic fashion with vegetables quickly tossed together on a tray. Given that we eat with our eyes first, I prefer a pretty circular pattern with alternating colourful vegetable rounds sitting on a bed of rich tomato sauce for a rockin' presentation. Beautiful, comforting, vegan and low carb, this one ticks all the boxes.

3 tablespoons extra-virgin olive oil, plus extra for drizzling

1 large onion, diced

handful of basil, leaves picked and roughly chopped, stalks finely chopped

sea salt flakes and freshly ground black pepper

4 garlic cloves, finely grated

400 g can chopped tomatoes

1 tablespoon balsamic vinegar

2 teaspoons thyme leaves, plus extra for sprinkling

1 teaspoon caster sugar

2 zucchini, cut into 1 cm-thick slices

2 Lebanese eggplants, cut into 1 cm-thick slices

3–4 long capsicums (mixed colours), deseeded and cut into 1 cm-thick slices

Preheat the oven to 200°C (fan-forced).

Combine the olive oil, onion and chopped basil stalks in a frying pan over low heat. Add a pinch of salt and sauté for 5 minutes or until the onion has softened. Add the garlic and cook for another 30 seconds.

Add the tomatoes, vinegar, thyme, sugar and chopped basil leaves and season to taste with salt and pepper. Simmer for 3 minutes to slightly reduce the sauce.

Pour the sauce into a 28 cm round baking dish. Create alternating stacks with the zucchini, eggplant and capsicum and arrange on their sides in a ring formation in the dish. Drizzle with extra olive oil and sprinkle with salt and extra thyme leaves.

Cover with baking paper, then foil and bake for 30 minutes. Remove the paper and foil and bake for another 30 minutes or until golden.

TIP
- Try to buy vegetables that are roughly the same shape and size so they stack neatly.

Quick Shredded Brussels Sprouts
WITH CRISPY PANCETTA

SERVES 4–6   DF, GF, LC

I hated brussels sprouts as a kid – they were always overboiled and just looked sad on my dinner plate. But now I know that if you quickly pan-fry them they are a textural delight with crispy brown edges and loads of crunch. Here, the salty pancetta fat and garlic impart a beautiful flavour and the hit of lemon at the end adds the perfect zing. A quick, easy and delicious veggie side dish your family will love, not hate.

100 g pancetta, diced
2 garlic cloves, finely grated
500 g brussels sprouts, finely shredded
  (preferably using a mandoline)
1 tablespoon extra-virgin olive oil
pinch of sea salt and freshly ground
  black pepper
juice of ½ lemon

Scatter the pancetta into a large cold frying pan. Place over medium-low heat and cook for 3–5 minutes until crisp. Add the garlic and cook for another 30 seconds.

Toss in the brussels sprouts and olive oil and season with salt and pepper. Sauté for 5 minutes or until the sprouts are crisp and bright green. Squeeze over the lemon juice and serve.

TIP

- If you add pancetta or bacon to a cold pan before placing over heat you will render out more of the fat and crisp the pancetta without burning it.

Amazing Asparagus
WITH LEEK, BACON & CRUSHED PISTACHIOS

SERVES 4–6   DF, GF, LC

Amazing is not an adjective often associated with greens, but when you partner asparagus with caramelised leek, salty bacon and crunchy pistachios the title is well earned. I love a slam-dunk side that can be tossed together in minutes, but this combination is so utterly delicious you could easily enjoy it as a main.

---

80 g bacon, diced

2 tablespoons extra-virgin olive oil

1 leek, white and light green parts, finely sliced

500 g asparagus, woody ends removed, diagonally cut into thirds

2 garlic cloves, finely grated

sea salt flakes and freshly ground black pepper

juice of 1 lemon, plus extra lemon wedges to serve

3 tablespoons pistachio kernels, toasted and crushed, to serve

Scatter the bacon into a large cold frying pan. Place over medium-low heat and cook for 3–5 minutes until crisp.

Increase the heat to medium, add the olive oil and leek and cook for 2 minutes. Add the asparagus and garlic, season with salt and pepper and cook for another 2 minutes.

Squeeze in the lemon juice and simmer for a minute or so until the asparagus is tender but still firm. Transfer to a platter, scatter over the crushed pistachios and serve with lemon wedges.

NOTE

• Asparagus and leeks are both great sources of fibre, folate, iron, antioxidants and other vitamins and minerals.

Roasted Beetroot
WITH SILKY SKORDALIA

SERVES 6–8   DF, GF, VG

Roasting is my favourite way to cook beetroot because it intensifies its natural sweetness for a more concentrated flavour than you get from steaming or boiling. A classic Greek accompaniment to roasted beetroot is skordalia, a silky smooth garlic potato dip that tastes sensational smothered over vegetables and crusty bread. Beetroot with skordalia features heavily in vegetarian banquets, particularly during Lent when many Greeks are following a vegan diet.

5 beetroot bulbs, stems and leaves removed
2 tablespoons extra-virgin olive oil, plus extra
  to serve
1 tablespoon white wine vinegar
pinch of sea salt flakes
flat-leaf parsley leaves, to serve
freshly ground black pepper

SKORDALIA

500 g sebago potatoes (or another floury
  variety), peeled and cut into 3 cm cubes
2 garlic cloves, finely grated
2 tablespoons white wine vinegar
pinch of sea salt flakes and ground
  white pepper
125 ml (½ cup) extra-virgin olive oil

Preheat the oven to 220°C (fan-forced).

Wrap the beetroot bulbs tightly in foil, place on a baking tray and roast for 1 hour or until cooked through. Remove the tray from the oven and set aside for 30 minutes so the beetroot sweats in the foil as it cools.

Meanwhile, to make the skordalia, place the potato in a saucepan of cold salted water. Bring to a simmer over low heat and cook for 15 minutes or until tender. Drain, reserving about 125 ml (½ cup) of the starchy water.

Transfer the hot potato to a food processor, add the garlic, vinegar, and salt and pepper and blitz to combine. With the motor running, slowly pour in the olive oil and 3 tablespoons of the reserved water to create a silky mash. Add a little more water if you prefer a thinner consistency. Spread the skordalia onto a platter.

Peel away the beetroot skins and slice into wedges. Toss in a bowl with the olive oil, vinegar and salt.

Arrange the beetroot on top of the skordalia, drizzle with olive oil, scatter over a few parsley leaves, season with pepper and serve.

PASTA & RICE

Slow-cooked
BEEF RAGU RIGATONI

SERVES 4–6   GF

Ragu needs to simmer for a few hours, but your patience will be well rewarded with tender, fall-apart beef in a rich tomato sauce. I consider this an essential pasta recipe that every home cook needs in their repertoire and it's actually very easy to make. Just remember to go low and slow. As a rule, it's best to serve robust sauces with a chunky pasta that can stand up to the rich flavours. I use rigatoni here, but any chunky pasta shape works.

700 g blade or chuck beef, cut into
   5 cm chunks
sea salt flakes and freshly ground black pepper
80 ml (⅓ cup) extra-virgin olive oil
1 onion, roughly chopped
1 large carrot, roughly chopped
1 celery stalk, roughly chopped
3 garlic cloves, finely grated
3 dried bay leaves
1 tablespoon chopped rosemary leaves
250 ml (1 cup) red wine
500 ml (2 cups) gluten-free beef stock
400 g can crushed tomatoes
2 tablespoons tomato paste
1 tablespoon balsamic vinegar
400 g gluten-free rigatoni
handful of basil leaves, chopped, plus a few
   extra small basil leaves, to serve
grated parmesan, to serve

Preheat the oven to 180°C (fan-forced).

Generously season the beef with salt and pepper. Heat 2 tablespoons of the olive oil in a large flameproof casserole dish over medium–high heat. Add the beef in batches and sear on all sides for 5 minutes or until nicely browned. Remove from the pan and set aside.

Reduce the heat to medium, add the remaining oil and sauté the onion, carrot and celery for 5 minutes or until softened. Add the garlic, bay leaves and rosemary and cook for another 30 seconds.

Pour in the red wine and simmer for 3 minutes or until reduced by half. Add the stock, crushed tomatoes, tomato paste and vinegar, then return the beef and resting juices to the dish and stir to combine. Bring to a simmer, then cover and transfer to the oven. Bake for 2 hours.

When the beef is almost ready, cook the rigatoni according to the packet instructions until al dente.

Remove the casserole from the oven and shred the meat with two forks. Stir through the basil. Using a large slotted spoon, transfer the pasta to the ragu, dragging some of the pasta water along for a silky sauce.

Divide the pasta and ragu among bowls and finish with grated cheese, basil leaves and a good grinding of pepper.

Garlic Prawns, Lime & Chilli
SUMMER SPAGHETTI

SERVES 4   DF, GF

Succulent garlic prawns spiked with chilli flakes and lime zest twirled with spaghetti scream summer
to me. This is the pasta I make after a long day at the beach when I want to refuel with something filling
but not too heavy. It comes together very quickly so make sure you have all your ingredients prepped
and ready to go. I leave the prawn tails intact for presentation but feel free to remove them
if you want to scoff faster.

350 g gluten-free spaghetti
3 tablespoons extra-virgin olive oil, plus
   extra for drizzling
3 garlic cloves, finely grated
¼ teaspoon dried chilli flakes
finely grated zest and juice of 1 lime, plus extra
   lime wedges to serve
20 large raw prawns, peeled and deveined,
   tails intact
sea salt flakes and freshly ground black pepper
handful of flat-leaf parsley leaves,
   finely chopped

Cook the spaghetti according to the packet instructions until
al dente.

Meanwhile, heat the olive oil in a large frying pan over
medium–low heat, add the garlic, chilli flakes and lime zest and
cook for 30 seconds. Add the prawns and a good pinch of salt and
pepper and cook for 2 minutes until they just turn opaque.

Using tongs, transfer the spaghetti directly into the pan, dragging
along some of the pasta water to create a silky sauce. Toss to
combine and cook for 1 minute, then add the lime juice and
parsley and toss again.

Divide the pasta among four plates, drizzle with extra olive oil,
finish with a grinding of pepper and serve with a wedge of lime.

Roasted Pumpkin, Rosemary
& GOAT'S CHEESE PASTA BAKE

SERVES 8 GF, V

In recent years I've made a conscious effort to feed my family more plant-based meals and this is one the kids absolutely love. Caramelised pumpkin, mushy peas and pasta tubes covered in creamy goat's cheese spiked with nutmeg and rosemary – what's not to love? A wholesome and nourishing pasta bake that is easy to make and a fantastic way to sneak extra veggies onto the plate. Mum win!

800 g kent pumpkin, peeled and cut into
  2 cm cubes
2 tablespoons extra-virgin olive oil
2 tablespoons chopped rosemary leaves
sea salt flakes and freshly ground black pepper
500 g gluten-free penne
155 g (1 cup) frozen or fresh peas
200 g creme fraiche
150 g goat's cheese, crumbled
pinch of grated nutmeg
100 g (1 cup) grated parmesan

Preheat the oven to 200°C (fan-forced).

Place the pumpkin in a 30 cm × 25 cm baking dish, add the olive oil, rosemary, 2 teaspoons salt and a good pinch of pepper and toss to combine. Roast, tossing halfway, for 40 minutes or until the pumpkin is tender and golden.

Cook the pasta according to the packet instructions until al dente. Drain, reserving about 3 tablespoons of the pasta water.

Add the pasta to the pumpkin, along with the peas, creme fraiche, goat's cheese, nutmeg and reserved water and gently toss to combine. Taste and season with more salt and pepper if required.

Sprinkle over the parmesan, then return to the oven and bake for 20 minutes or until the top is golden and crunchy.

Cherry Tomato & Basil Casarecce
WITH CASHEW PARMESAN

SERVES 4–6   DF, GF, VG

When I was on a strict eight-week detox last year my naturopath advised me to completely eliminate dairy from my diet so I started making vegan cheese at home to sprinkle over my pasta. It mimics parmesan in flavour and texture so closely that I even had my cheese-loving husband fooled. He loved it! My favourite pasta combinations are simple ones with an olive oil base, and this traditional cherry tomato and basil dish fits the bill. Perfect for a light summer lunch.

3 tablespoons extra-virgin olive oil
1 large onion, finely chopped
sea salt flakes and freshly ground black pepper
2 garlic cloves, finely grated
handful of basil, leaves picked and torn, stalks finely chopped
400 g gluten-free casarecce
250 g cherry tomatoes, halved
100 ml white wine

CASHEW PARMESAN
80 g (½ cup) raw cashews
2 tablespoons nutritional yeast flakes (see Notes)
1 teaspoon sea salt flakes
¼ teaspoon garlic powder

To make the cashew parmesan, process all the ingredients in a food processor, or use a mortar and pestle to grind the mixture until it resembles grated parmesan. Store in an airtight container in the fridge – it will keep for up to 3 weeks.

Heat the olive oil in a large frying pan over medium–low heat, add the onion and a pinch of salt and sauté for 5 minutes or until softened. Stir in the garlic and basil stalks and cook for another 30 seconds.

Meanwhile, cook the pasta according to the packet instructions until al dente.

Add the cherry tomatoes and another pinch of salt to the onion mixture and cook for 3 minutes until they start to blister. Pour in the wine and simmer, stirring to release any caramelised bits caught on the base of the pan, for 3 minutes or until slightly reduced.

Drain the pasta, reserving some of the cooking water. Add the pasta to the tomato mixture, along with a few splashes of the cooking water to create a silky sauce. Toss to combine for 1 minute.

Divide the pasta among bowls and top with the torn basil leaves and a grinding of pepper. Finish with a sprinkling of cashew parmesan.

NOTES
- Nutritional yeast flakes are a great source of protein, B vitamins and minerals. They can be found in the health-food aisle of the supermarket or in health-food stores.

- You can replace the cashews with macadamias or sunflower seeds. Just be aware that the cheese will have a slightly different taste and texture.

Best-ever
BEEF LASAGNE

SERVES 6–8 GF

When I first moved out of home, lasagne was my go-to dish when hosting dinner parties because I could make it with my eyes closed and it never let me down. I have such a deep affection for lasagne it would probably be my death-row dish. Golden cheesy bechamel aside, I amp the sauce up with pancetta, red wine, cinnamon and nutmeg. Trust me, these little aromatic additions will make this your best-ever lasagne.

3 tablespoons extra-virgin olive oil
1 onion, finely chopped
1 carrot, finely chopped
1 celery stalk, finely chopped
sea salt flakes and freshly ground black pepper
2 garlic cloves, finely grated
150 g pancetta, finely diced
500 g beef mince
2 tablespoons tomato paste
2 x 400 g cans crushed tomatoes
125 ml (½ cup) red wine
1 teaspoon dried oregano
1 cinnamon stick
pinch of grated nutmeg
handful of basil leaves, finely chopped
200 g gluten-free lasagne sheets
grated parmesan, for layering

BECHAMEL
100 g butter
100 g gluten-free plain flour
800 ml full-cream milk
100 g parmesan, grated
1 egg, whisked
pinch of ground cinnamon
pinch of sea salt

Heat the olive oil in a large saucepan over medium–low heat, add the onion, carrot, celery and a pinch of salt and sauté for 5 minutes or until softened. Add the garlic and pancetta and sauté for another 30 seconds.

Add the mince and brown for 2–3 minutes, breaking it up with a wooden spoon. Stir in the tomato paste and cook for another minute.

Add the crushed tomatoes, wine, oregano, cinnamon and nutmeg, and season with salt and pepper. Cover and simmer over low heat for 1 hour or until the sauce is thick and rich. Taste and season with more salt and pepper if necessary, then stir in the basil. Set aside.

Preheat the oven to 180°C (fan-forced) and grease a large rectangular baking dish with olive oil.

For the bechamel, melt the butter in a small saucepan over low heat, then stir in the flour to form a smooth paste. Cook off the flour for 30 seconds, then slowly pour in the milk, stirring constantly, to create a thick bechamel. Add the cheese and stir to melt and combine. Remove the pan from the heat and whisk in the egg and cinnamon. Season to taste with salt.

To assemble the lasagne, spread a thin layer of bolognese over the base of the baking dish and place a single layer of lasagne sheets on the sauce. Top with more bolognese and a layer of bechamel, then a sprinkling of extra cheese. Repeat the layers with the remaining ingredients, finishing with a final layer of bechamel and cheese, then bake for 45 minutes or until golden.

TIP
- Assemble your lasagne the day before and let it sit in the fridge uncooked to intensify the flavours. Pop it in the oven before your guests arrive so you can entertain with ease.

Speedy Lemon–Tuna
BOW TIES

SERVES 4   DF, GF

This is the pasta dish I make for my kids when the fridge is empty and I need to get a speedy dinner on the table using a few pantry staples. Canned tuna is extremely versatile and a cheap source of healthy protein – I always have plenty in the cupboard for last-minute meal ideas. The pepper and parsley are not essential here. Leave them out if you want to keep the pasta simple for kids like my daughter, Ruby, who always requests 'no green leaves'.

250 g gluten-free bow tie pasta
3 tablespoons extra-virgin olive oil
1 small onion, diced
pinch of sea salt flakes and freshly ground
  black pepper
2 garlic cloves, finely grated
3 x 95 g cans tuna in spring water, drained
zest and juice of ½ lemon
handful of flat-leaf parsley leaves,
  finely chopped

Cook the pasta according to the packet instructions until al dente.

When the pasta is almost ready, heat the olive oil in a large frying pan over medium heat. Add the onion and a pinch of salt and sauté for 2–3 minutes until softened, then add the garlic and cook for 30 seconds. Add the tuna, breaking it up with a wooden spoon.

Using a slotted spoon, transfer the pasta directly into the pan, dragging along some of the pasta water to create a silky sauce. Toss to combine and cook for another minute. Add the lemon zest and juice, parsley and some pepper and toss again.

Divide the pasta among bowls and serve.

Lamb Pastitsio

SERVES 6–8   GF

Pastitsio is Greece's answer to lasagne. The rich bolognese sauce is infused with an aromatic combination of oregano, rosemary, cinnamon and my favourite spice in tomato sauces … nutmeg! You then toss the bolognese with some gluten-free penne before smothering it with a cheesy bechamel for the ultimate winter comfort bake. I usually add whisked egg to my bechamel to give it a silky finish, and remember to always cook off the flour when whisking so you're not left with a floury aftertaste.

3 tablespoons extra-virgin olive oil
1 onion, finely chopped
2 garlic cloves, roughly chopped
500 g lamb mince
1 teaspoon dried oregano
1 tablespoon chopped rosemary leaves
2 x 400 g cans crushed tomatoes
2 tablespoons tomato paste
1 cinnamon stick
pinch of grated nutmeg
sea salt flakes and freshly ground black pepper
300 g gluten-free penne
grated kefalograviera cheese, for sprinkling

BECHAMEL
100 g butter
100 g gluten-free plain flour
800 ml full-cream milk
100 g kefalograviera cheese, grated
100 g parmesan, grated
1 egg, whisked
pinch of ground cinnamon
pinch of sea salt

Heat the olive oil in a large saucepan over medium–low heat, add the onion and sauté for 5 minutes or until softened. Add the garlic and cook for another 30 seconds.

Add the mince, oregano and rosemary and brown for 2–3 minutes, breaking up the mince with a wooden spoon.

Add the crushed tomatoes, tomato paste, cinnamon stick, nutmeg and a generous pinch of salt and pepper. Cover and simmer over low heat for 1 hour or until thick and rich.

Preheat the oven to 200°C (fan-forced) and grease a large rectangular baking dish with olive oil.

When the sauce is almost ready, cook the pasta according to the packet instructions until al dente. Drain, then transfer the penne to the prepared baking dish. Remove the cinnamon stick, then pour over the bolognese sauce and toss to combine.

For the bechamel, melt the butter in a small saucepan over low heat, then stir in the flour to form a smooth paste. Cook off the flour for 30 seconds, then slowly pour in the milk, stirring constantly to create a thick bechamel. Add the cheeses and stir to melt and combine. Remove the pan from the heat and whisk in the egg and cinnamon. Season to taste with salt.

Spread the bechamel over the pasta mixture and sprinkle with kefalograviera. Bake for 40 minutes or until golden.

Spinach & Ricotta Ravioli
WITH SAGE & BURNT BUTTER SAUCE

SERVES 4–6 GF, V

Ravioli can be intimidating for the home cook; add the gluten-free factor and most wouldn't bother. The basic principles of pasta making are actually the same – the dough is just more delicate and less stretchy so it requires a gentle hand. Handmade ravioli is not something you'd whip up mid week but it's a skill worth learning because these tender pillows are a thing of beauty. My preferred flour for gluten-free pasta dough is brown rice flour because it is gritty and helps the dough hold its structure. Fill with a classic spinach and ravioli combo and dress with a simple buttery sauce for an impressive plate of restaurant-quality pasta.

100 g butter
12 sage leaves
toasted pine nuts and grated parmesan,
    to serve

PASTA DOUGH
280 g (2 cups) brown rice flour
80 g (⅔ cup) tapioca flour, plus extra
    for dusting
1½ teaspoons xanthan gum
½ teaspoon sea salt
5 eggs

FILLING
250 g baby spinach leaves, finely chopped
300 g full-fat ricotta
100 g parmesan, finely grated
finely grated zest of ½ lemon
pinch of grated nutmeg
pinch of sea salt and freshly ground
    black pepper

TIPS FOR PERFECT RAVIOLI
- Roll the dough as thinly as possible so you have delicate pillows, not thick chewy dough. You want to be able to see the shadow of your hand behind the dough. If your pasta sheets start to tear, this is a good indication you should stop at the previous setting on your machine.

- If your dough sheet becomes too long during rolling, cut it in half to make it easier to handle.

- It's important that you remove any air bubbles. Trapped air will cause the pillows to rupture and leak.

To make the pasta dough, combine the flours, xanthan gum and salt in a mixing bowl. Add the eggs and beat until a dough forms. Press the dough into a disc, wrap in plastic wrap and refrigerate for 30 minutes to firm up.

Meanwhile, prepare the filling. Place the spinach leaves in a large frying pan, add 3 tablespoons of water and cook for 2–3 minutes until wilted. Drain the spinach, then firmly squeeze out the excess moisture and roughly chop. Transfer the spinach to a bowl, add the remaining ingredients and stir to combine.

Divide the dough into five portions and dust with tapioca flour. Working with one piece at a time, flatten the dough into a rectangle the same width as the rollers of your pasta machine. Start rolling the dough through on the widest setting. Initially the dough will look dry and brittle but keep going. Fold the pasta sheet into an envelope shape and roll through the machine at the same setting three or four times to smooth it out. Reduce the setting each time you roll until the dough is nice and thin – usually setting 6, depending on your machine. If the pasta gets sticky between rolls, dust with extra tapioca flour. Roll out the remaining dough.

Place a sheet of baking paper on the work bench and top with the pasta sheet. Place 1½ teaspoons of filling at 4 cm intervals along the centre of the sheet. Brush a little water around the filling and top with another sheet of pasta. Gently press with your fingers to remove any air bubbles and seal, then cut out ravioli with a 6 cm round cutter. Repeat with the remaining pasta and filling.

Cook the ravioli in a large saucepan of gently simmering salted water for 7–8 minutes. Remove with a slotted spoon and divide evenly among plates.

Meanwhile, melt the butter in a frying pan over medium heat for 2 minutes until foamy and nut brown. Add the sage leaves and fry for 20 seconds until crisp. Spoon the butter sauce over the ravioli, sprinkle over pine nuts and cheese and serve immediately.

Walnut & Rosemary
PESTO SPIRALS

SERVES 4 GF, V

Busy weeknights call for simple pasta dishes that can be pulled together in a flash. This delicious pesto is my midweek saviour because I always have nuts stocked in my pantry and rosemary grows wild in my garden all year round. The walnuts can be swapped for any nut of your choice, or for a nut-free version use pumpkins seeds or perhaps try a green olive pesto.

350 g gluten-free spiral pasta
your favourite grated cheese and freshly
  ground black pepper, to serve

WALNUT & ROSEMARY PESTO
100 g (1 cup) walnuts
2 tablespoons rosemary leaves
100 ml extra-virgin olive oil
1 garlic clove, roughly chopped
2 anchovy fillets
1 teaspoon sea salt flakes
pinch of freshly ground black pepper
40 g your favourite cheese, grated

Cook the pasta according to the packet instructions until al dente.

Meanwhile, to make the walnut and rosemary pesto, blitz the ingredients in a food processor to form a chunky paste (or use a mortar and pestle). Transfer the pesto to a large frying pan.

When the pasta is almost ready, warm the pesto over low heat for a minute or so. Using a slotted spoon, transfer the pasta directly into the pan, dragging along some of the pasta water to loosen the pesto and create a silky sauce. Stir until the pasta is well coated in the pesto.

Top with grated cheese and a grinding of pepper and serve.

TIP
- Rosemary is a great choice to start a herb garden with because it is so sturdy. It loves sun or shade and will not die in the winter months so you can season your food with its distinctive pinewood flavour all year round.

Spaghetti
WITH PORK & VEAL MEATBALLS

SERVES 4 GF

If there's one thing I really dislike it's a tough meatball. To get them light and fluffy it's best to add a starchy component to your mince mixture. Traditionally, Italian nonnas use breadcrumbs soaked in milk but in my gluten-free meatballs I add a finely grated floury potato and it works a treat. It's best to use two types of mince for a well-rounded flavour – pork and veal is my favourite combo but you could also use beef or chicken if you prefer. With its aromatic pine notes, sage complements pork beautifully, but it has quite an assertive flavour so use it sparingly.

extra-virgin olive oil, for pan-frying
   and drizzling
350 g gluten-free spaghetti
your favourite grated cheese and
   flat-leaf parsley leaves, to serve
freshly ground black pepper

MEATBALLS
250 g veal mince
250 g pork mince
1 sebago potato (or another floury variety),
   peeled and very finely grated, excess
   moisture squeezed out
2 garlic cloves, finely grated
1 egg
small handful of flat-leaf parsley leaves,
   finely chopped
2 tablespoons finely chopped sage leaves
generous pinch of sea salt flakes and
   freshly ground black pepper

SAUCE
1 tablespoon extra-virgin olive oil
1 onion, finely chopped
400 ml passata
125 ml (½ cup) red wine
small handful of basil leaves, chopped
pinch of grated nutmeg
sea salt flakes and freshly ground black pepper

To make the meatballs, place the ingredients in a bowl and mix well with your hands. Refrigerate for 30 minutes to firm up, then roll into about 16 meatballs.

Heat a good splash of olive oil in a large frying pan over medium–high heat. Sear the meatballs for 2–3 minutes, constantly rotating them in the pan until golden. Remove the meatballs from the pan and set aside.

For the sauce, heat the olive oil in the pan over medium heat, add the onion and sauté for 2–3 minutes until softened. Scrape the bottom of the pan to release any caramelised bits from the meatballs. Add the remaining sauce ingredients along with 3 tablespoons of water and stir to combine. Taste and adjust the seasoning if necessary.

Return the meatballs to the pan, then cover and simmer for 20 minutes or until the meatballs are cooked through and the sauce has thickened.

Meanwhile, cook the spaghetti according to the packet instructions until al dente. Drain, then add to the pan with the meatballs and sauce.

To serve, divide the spaghetti, meatballs and sauce among bowls, top with cheese and parsley and finish with a grinding of pepper.

Simple Midweek
FRIED RICE

SERVES 6   DF, GF

Speedy fried rice is always on high rotation in our home. I love the combination of crispy bacon, carrot and egg but once you get the basic ingredients right you can add whatever protein or veggies you like. Prawns, tofu or shredded chicken are a nice addition for a complete meal, and if you want to make this vegan simply omit the bacon and egg.

3 tablespoons peanut oil

3 eggs, whisked

3 rindless bacon rashers, finely diced

1 carrot, finely diced

1 small onion, finely chopped

1 teaspoon finely grated ginger

1 garlic clove, finely grated

2 tablespoons dry sherry

925 g (5 cups) cooked jasmine rice, cooled (see page 21 and Tip)

1 teaspoon sesame oil

2 tablespoons gluten-free tamari or coconut aminos

3 spring onions, finely sliced, a few slices reserved to serve

Place a wok over high heat and add 1 tablespoon of the peanut oil. Pour in the egg and cook for 1 minute, then fold it over like an omelette, transfer to a chopping board and slice into strips.

Heat the remaining oil in the wok, add the bacon, carrot, onion, ginger and garlic and stir-fry for 4 minutes. Pour in the sherry and stir for another minute to release any caramelised bits caught on the base of the wok.

Add the rice, sesame oil and tamari or coconut aminos and stir-fry for 2–3 minutes to combine and heat through. Return the egg to the wok, add the spring onion and toss well. Serve immediately topped with extra spring onion.

TIP

- It is best to use cold day-old rice that has dehydrated in the fridge overnight for a crispy texture. If you have not prepared rice the day before, just pop your cooked rice in the fridge to cool so it's not gluggy.

Chicken Teriyaki
SUSHI SANDWICHES

MAKES 1   DF, GF

When I can't decide between a sandwich or sushi for lunch I make 'onigirazo', or sushi sandwiches. They are much easier to assemble than sushi rolls – you just flatten your sticky rice to resemble bread slices and fill away. Vary the fillings to suit your tastes; for example, replace the chicken with cooked prawns or omit the chicken altogether and make a vegetarian cucumber option. Perfectly portable, these super-healthy Instagram-worthy sandwiches will definitely not go soggy in your lunchbox. I give instructions for making one sandwich here, but you can obviously multiply this by the number of mouths you have to feed.

1 tablespoon extra-virgin olive oil
1 skinless chicken thigh fillet, flattened with your fist or a rolling pin
3 tablespoons gluten-free teriyaki sauce
1 nori sheet
185 g (1 cup) cooked sushi rice (see page 21)
a few butter lettuce leaves
1 carrot, julienned
toasted sesame seeds

JAPANESE MAYONNAISE
2 egg yolks
1 garlic clove, finely grated
1 teaspoon gluten-free tamari or coconut aminos
1 teaspoon dijon mustard
2 teaspoons apple cider vinegar
pinch of sea salt flakes and ground white pepper
200 ml light olive oil

To make the Japanese mayonnaise, place the egg yolks, garlic, tamari or coconut aminos, mustard, vinegar, salt and pepper in a blender and whiz to combine. With the motor running, very slowly add the oil in a thin stream until the mayonnaise starts to emulsify. Pour the mayonnaise into a squeeze bottle and store in the fridge for up to 2 weeks.

Heat the olive oil in a frying pan over medium heat, add the chicken and cook for 3–4 minutes on each side or until golden and cooked through. In the last minute pour in the teriyaki sauce to glaze the chicken, then remove and set aside to rest. Leave it whole if you like, or finely slice it.

To assemble the sandwich, place the nori on a piece of plastic wrap in a diamond shape with the rough side facing upwards. Add half the rice and shape into a square in the centre of the nori, pressing down to slightly flatten. Layer the lettuce, carrot, chicken, mayonnaise and sesame seeds on top and finish with the remaining rice, again in a square shape.

Fold in the corners of the nori sheet to enclose the sandwich, and firmly wrap with plastic wrap. Leave for 10 minutes to allow the nori to soften before slicing. Sprinkle with extra sesame seeds.

Spanakorizo
(SPINACH PILAF)

SERVES 4   DF, GF, VG

Spanakorizo is a traditional Greek spinach and rice pilaf. I have fond memories of gobbling up bowls of this nourishing dish as a kid – the spoon was often larger than my hungry little mouth. Very simple to prepare yet so nutrient dense with all those antioxidant-rich leafy greens. Serve it as is for a beautiful vegan meal, or add crumbled Greek feta, a dollop of yoghurt or a poached egg for a lovely vegetarian brunch.

3 tablespoons extra-virgin olive oil
1 small onion, chopped
1 garlic clove, finely grated
1 large bunch of English spinach, trimmed,
    thoroughly washed, leaves roughly chopped
3 spring onions, finely sliced
200 g canned chopped tomatoes or
    1 large tomato, chopped
sea salt flakes and freshly ground black pepper
100 g (½ cup) medium-grain rice, rinsed
    and drained
Greek feta, to serve (optional)
lemon wedges, to serve

Heat the olive oil in a large saucepan over medium heat, add the onion and sauté for 3 minutes or until softened. Add the garlic, spinach, spring onion, tomato, salt and pepper and cook for another 2 minutes.

Add the rice and 500 ml (2 cups) of water. Reduce the heat to low and simmer, covered, for 20 minutes or until the rice is tender, adding a splash more water if required. Taste and adjust the seasoning if needed, crumble over a little feta (if using), then serve with lemon wedges.

SEAFOOD

Sofia's Healthy
CRUMBED FISH FINGERS

SERVES 4–6 DF, GF, LC

My eldest daughter Sofia loves fish but hates greasy food so I decided to give fish fingers a healthy makeover. Just swap your oily frying pan for a baking tray and you'll have the most delicious and nutritious crumbed fish in no time. Flathead is my preferred fish here because it is super light and flaky – a real winner with the kids. A little mustard in your whisked eggs amps up the flavour – that's my secret tip for the best (and healthiest) fish fingers in the world.

40 g (⅓ cup) tapioca flour
2 eggs
2 tablespoons dijon mustard
90 g (1¼ cups) gluten-free breadcrumbs
handful of flat-leaf parsley leaves,
    finely chopped
1 tablespoon sea salt flakes
pinch of ground white pepper
600 g flathead fillets, skin and bones
    removed, each cut into 2–3 pieces
extra-virgin olive oil, for drizzling
lemon wedges, to serve

Preheat the oven to 200°C (fan-forced) and brush a baking tray with olive oil.

Before you start crumbing you need to set up three stations: tapioca flour in one bowl, whisked eggs and mustard in another, and the breadcrumbs, parsley, salt and pepper in a third.

Individually dip each piece of fish in tapioca flour, dusting off the excess, then in the eggy mustard, and then firmly press into the breadcrumb mixture to coat on all sides.

Place the fish fingers on the prepared tray in a single layer and drizzle with olive oil (or use oil spray if you prefer). Bake for 10–12 minutes or until golden and cooked through. Serve with lemon wedges.

Prawn Saganaki

SERVES 4   GF, LC

Prawn saganaki is an iconic Greek entree of succulent prawns simmered in a rich tomato sauce, topped with chunks of oozy, melted feta. Super easy to prepare and perfect for entertaining, your guests will be impressed when the rustic pan hits the table. This is the dish that immediately transports you back to that stunning summer holiday on the Greek islands.

3 tablespoons extra-virgin olive oil,
   plus extra to serve
2 large onions, finely sliced
sea salt flakes and freshly ground black pepper
3 garlic cloves, finely grated
pinch of dried chilli flakes
2 tablespoons tomato paste
125 ml (½ cup) white wine
400 g can chopped tomatoes
700 g raw prawns (roughly 20 prawns),
   peeled and deveined, tails intact
100 g Greek feta
handful of flat-leaf parsley leaves,
   finely chopped
Easy Bowl & Spoon Gluten-free Loaf
   (page 29), to serve (optional)

Heat the olive oil in a large, shallow oven-safe frying pan over low heat, add the onion and a pinch of salt and cook for 5 minutes or until softened. Add the garlic, chilli flakes and tomato paste and cook for another 30 seconds, stirring to combine.

Pour in the wine and simmer for 2–3 minutes until reduced by half. Add the chopped tomatoes and a generous pinch of salt and pepper and simmer for 5 minutes to thicken the sauce.

Add the prawns to the pan, stir to combine and crumble chunks of feta on top. Place the pan under a hot grill for 5 minutes or until the prawns are cooked and the feta has melted.

Take the pan to the table. Drizzle with extra olive oil, sprinkle with parsley and serve with crusty gluten-free bread, if you like.

Sensational
SNAPPER PIES

SERVES 4   DF, GF

Traditionally fish pies are loaded with dairy for creaminess, but not this one! My snapper pie is super creamy and guests are always shocked to discover it's completely dairy free. I use coconut cream instead and it works beautifully, though you actually can't taste the coconut at all. Caramelising the onions at the beginning concentrates their natural sweetness for added intensity and the sauce is finished with wine, mustard and thyme for a sensational flavour burst.

2–3 small sebago potatoes (or another floury variety), peeled and finely sliced (preferably using a mandoline)

3 tablespoons extra-virgin olive oil, plus extra for brushing

3 large onions, finely sliced

sea salt flakes and ground white pepper

180 ml (¾ cup) white wine

375 ml (1½ cups) coconut cream

1 tablespoon dijon mustard

2 teaspoons thyme leaves, plus extra for sprinkling

600 g snapper fillet, skin and bones removed, cut into 4 cm chunks

150 g (1 cup) frozen peas

handful of flat-leaf parsley leaves, finely chopped

Steam the potato slices in a steamer basket over simmering water for 10 minutes or until softened, then transfer to a wire rack to cool and dry.

Meanwhile, heat the olive oil in a large frying pan over low heat, add the onion and a pinch of salt and gently sauté for 15 minutes to caramelise, stirring regularly to prevent burning.

Pour in the wine and simmer for 2–3 minutes until reduced by half. Add the coconut cream, mustard, thyme and a pinch of pepper and simmer for 5 minutes or until thickened. Pour the mixture into a food processor and puree to a smooth, creamy sauce.

Preheat the oven to 200°C (fan forced).

Divide half the sauce evenly among four 375 ml (1½ cup) capacity pie dishes or ramekins. Place the fish on top and sprinkle over the peas and parsley, then pour over the remaining sauce. Arrange the potato slices in a circular pattern on top.

Brush with extra olive oil, sprinkle with salt and bake for 25–30 minutes or until the fish is tender, then place the pies under the oven grill and cook for another 5 minutes or until the potato is crisp and golden. Sprinkle over extra thyme leaves before serving.

Singapore
PRAWN ZOODLES

SERVES 2   DF, GF, LC

All the signature flavours of Singapore noodles minus the gluten, starch ... and guilt! I've given
a traditionally calorie-laden takeaway meal a healthy and delicious makeover and it only takes minutes
to toss together. Zucchini noodles are a great option for those watching their carb intake, and can
replace starchy noodles, pasta or rice in any dish. Just pick up a cheap spiraliser at any kitchenware store
and get zoodling. It's a great way to make veggies fun and playful for the entire family. By all means
increase the quantities to serve more people, but cook it in batches so you don't overcrowd the wok,
causing the ingredients to stew.

2 tablespoons coconut oil

2 eggs, whisked

1 small onion, finely sliced

1 teaspoon finely grated ginger

1 garlic clove, finely grated

1 small red capsicum, deseeded and
    finely sliced

100 g green beans, trimmed and halved

2 teaspoons gluten-free curry powder

1 tablespoon gluten-free tamari or
    coconut aminos

2 teaspoons fish sauce

12 raw prawns, peeled and deveined,
    tails intact

2 zucchini, spiralised

juice of 1 small lime

coriander sprigs, to serve

Melt 1 tablespoon of the coconut oil in a large wok over medium–
high heat, pour in the egg and cook for 1 minute, then fold it over
like an omelette, transfer to a chopping board and slice into strips.
Set aside.

Melt the remaining oil in the wok, add the onion, ginger, garlic,
capsicum and beans and stir-fry for 3 minutes or until softened. Add
the curry powder, tamari or coconut aminos and fish sauce and toss
through the vegetables. Add the prawns and stir-fry for 1 minute or
until they turn pink.

Return the egg strips to the wok, add the zucchini spirals and squeeze
over the lime juice. Stir-fry for 2 minutes to combine the flavours,
then serve straight away with coriander scattered over the top.

NOTE

- Zucchini is low in carbs, high in fibre and antioxidants, and contains
significant amounts of vitamins A, C and K.

Crispy Salt & Pepper Squid
WITH MINT & PARSLEY

SERVES 4–6   DF, GF, LC

I rarely eat fried food but crispy salt and pepper squid is one dish I can't resist. I always order two servings at a restaurant because my daughter Sofia devours a whole plate while the rest of us happily share the other. You can dust your squid in either tapioca flour or potato starch – tapioca will give you a lighter, crisper finish, while potato starch results in a thicker, crunchier coating. Both are delicious, especially when sprinkled with fresh mint and parsley and a good squeeze of lemon juice.

120 g (1 cup) tapioca flour or 160 g (1 cup) potato starch
1 tablespoon sea salt flakes
1 teaspoon freshly ground black pepper
2 egg whites
5 whole squid (roughly 1 kg), cleaned, tentacles removed, hoods sliced into 1 cm rings and flat pieces scored
extra-virgin olive oil, for deep-frying
handful of mint leaves, finely chopped
handful of flat-leaf parsley leaves, finely chopped
lemon wedges, to serve

Combine the flour, salt and pepper in a shallow bowl. Whisk the egg whites in a second bowl.

Dip the squid in the egg white, allowing the excess to drip off, then coat well in the flour, dusting off the excess.

Heat enough olive oil for deep-frying in a large, deep frying pan until it reaches 180°C on a kitchen thermometer (or until a cube of gluten-free bread dropped in the oil browns in 15 seconds). Add the squid in batches (so you don't overcrowd the pan) and cook for 1–2 minutes or until crisp and lightly golden. Remove with a slotted spoon and drain on a wire rack with paper towel underneath to stop the squid going soggy.

Finish with the fresh herbs, sprinkle with salt and serve hot with lemon wedges.

Fish
EN PAPILLOTE

SERVES 4   DF, GF, LC

Cooking fish 'en papillote' means to bake it wrapped in baking paper. This is a foolproof method if you are concerned about overcooking fish as the steam trapped inside the paper parcel keeps it wonderfully moist. The Mediterranean flavours of wine, lemon, tomato and olives make the dish light but super flavoursome. My kids love unwrapping their little parcels when they hit the dinner table – it's like Christmas all year round!

3 tablespoons extra-virgin olive oil
3 tablespoons white wine
juice of 1 small lemon
12 cherry tomatoes, halved
12 Sicilian olives
2 spring onions, finely sliced
handful of flat-leaf parsley leaves
4 x 200 g white fish fillets (such as barramundi or john dory), skin and bones removed
sea salt flakes and freshly ground black pepper

Preheat the oven to 200°C (fan-forced). Lay out four 30 cm × 20 cm sheets of baking paper on the work bench, then place another sheet on each to create a double layer (a double layer guarantees a tight seal). Scrunch up the baking paper so the sides sit up to create a nest shape.

In a bowl, combine the olive oil, white wine, lemon juice, tomato, olives, spring onion and parsley.

Place one fish fillet in the centre of each paper nest and season with salt and pepper. Spoon the tomato mixture onto each fillet and fold the first sheet of baking paper over the fish, twisting the ends to make a parcel. Repeat with the second sheet for a tight seal.

Place the four parcels on a baking tray and bake for 12 minutes, depending on the size of the fillets – thicker pieces will need a little longer. To check if the fish is cooked through, gently open one parcel to ensure the fish is opaque white. If not, cook for another few minutes and check again.

Place the parcels on plates and open them at the table (be careful of the hot steam).

Ruby's
ASIAN GLAZED SALMON

SERVES 4   DF, GF, LC

My youngest daughter Ruby is obsessed with salmon and requests it for dinner at least once a week. Her favourite marinade only requires a few ingredients and the sticky glaze caramelises beautifully under a hot grill. With sticky glazes I find the safest method is to grill the fish in the oven otherwise the sugars can burn in the frying pan leaving you with a black crust and raw fish. If you have time, marinate the fish overnight so the flavours can mingle and intensify – you will definitely taste the difference.

3 tablespoons gluten-free tamari or
  coconut aminos
2 tablespoons mirin
1 tablespoon raw honey
1 tablespoon finely grated ginger
2 garlic cloves, finely grated
4 x 200 g salmon fillets, skin and
  bones removed

TO SERVE
sliced spring onion, lime wedges and toasted
  sesame seeds (optional)
cooked jasmine rice (see page 21)

Combine the tamari or coconut aminos, mirin, honey, ginger and garlic in a glass or ceramic dish or tray. Add the salmon and turn to coat in the marinade. Marinate in the fridge for at least 1 hour or preferably overnight.

Place the salmon on a lined tray. Pour the remaining marinade into a small saucepan.

Grill the salmon for 6–9 minutes until it is caramelised on top and cooked to your liking (6 minutes for medium, up to 9 minutes for well done).

When the salmon is almost ready, simmer the marinade in the pan for 2–3 minutes to thicken to a glaze. Brush the glaze over the cooked salmon. Finish with spring onion, lime wedges and sesame seeds (if using) and serve with rice.

NOTE
• Salmon is high in protein, low in carbs and rich in heart-healthy omega-3s.

Tender
CHARGRILLED OCTOPUS

SERVES 4   DF, GF, LC

The idea of cooking octopus can be daunting if you've never done it before as it can so often turn out tough or rubbery. Relax; my simple two-step method works every time, resulting in a soft, juicy interior and a crispy charred exterior. The key is to first simmer the octopus with aromatics to tenderise and flavour the meat before bathing it in extra-virgin olive oil to chargrill. Just one golden rule: be careful not to overcook the octopus when simmering or it will turn to mush.

250 ml (1 cup) red wine vinegar
4 garlic cloves, peeled
3 dried bay leaves
juice of 1 lemon
1 tablespoon sea salt flakes, plus extra if needed
1 kg large octopus, cleaned
pinch of dried oregano
pinch of freshly ground black pepper
extra-virgin olive oil, for drizzling
lemon wedges, to serve

Pour 3 litres of water into a large saucepan. Add the vinegar, garlic, bay leaves, lemon juice and salt and bring to the boil. Reduce the heat to low, add the octopus and simmer gently for 40 minutes or until fork tender. Remove the octopus and set aside to cool to room temperature.

Cut the octopus into large tentacle sections. Peel away any loose hanging skin, being careful to keep the suckers intact, and place the octopus in a bowl. Taste a small piece and add more salt if needed, along with the oregano and pepper. Drizzle a generous amount of olive oil over the octopus, then turn to coat in the seasoned oil.

Heat a chargrill pan or barbecue grill plate until smoking hot. Grill the octopus for 2–3 minutes each side until charred. Serve the tentacles whole or cut into pieces with lemon wedges.

Sesame-crusted Cod,
SOBA NOODLES &
TAMARI-GINGER DRESSING

SERVES 4   DF, GF

Cod is a mild, flaky fish that comes to life when paired with flavoursome dressings and contrasting textures. The cod fillets only take a few minutes to cook in the pan and form a golden sesame crust. While the fish is resting, quickly boil the soba noodles, whisk the tangy Asian dressing and your family will be vigorously slurping on their zesty noodles in no time at all.

4 x 200 g cod fillets, skin and bones removed, at room temperature
1 teaspoon sea salt flakes
pinch of freshly ground black pepper
115 g (¾ cup) sesame seeds (combination of white and black)
1 tablespoon extra-virgin olive oil
300 g gluten-free soba noodles
120 g snow peas, trimmed
spring onion, shredded, to serve

TAMARI-GINGER DRESSING
3 tablespoons gluten-free tamari or coconut aminos
3 tablespoons mirin
2 teaspoons finely grated ginger
2 teaspoons raw honey
1 teaspoon toasted sesame oil
1 garlic clove, finely grated
juice of 1 lime

Season the fish with the salt and pepper. Place the sesame seeds on a tray or plate. Firmly press the cod fillets into the sesame seeds to coat well all over.

Heat the olive oil in a large frying pan over medium–high heat, add the cod and pan-fry for 2–3 minutes on each side until the sesame seeds are golden. Remove and rest on a wire rack.

Meanwhile, cook the soba noodles in a saucepan of boiling water for 6 minutes, adding the snow peas for the last 30 seconds to quickly blanch them. Drain and rinse well under cold water, separating the noodles with your hands.

To make the dressing, whisk the ingredients in a small bowl.

Divide the noodles and snow peas among four shallow bowls and spoon over the dressing. Place one cod fillet in each bowl, sprinkle with spring onion and serve.

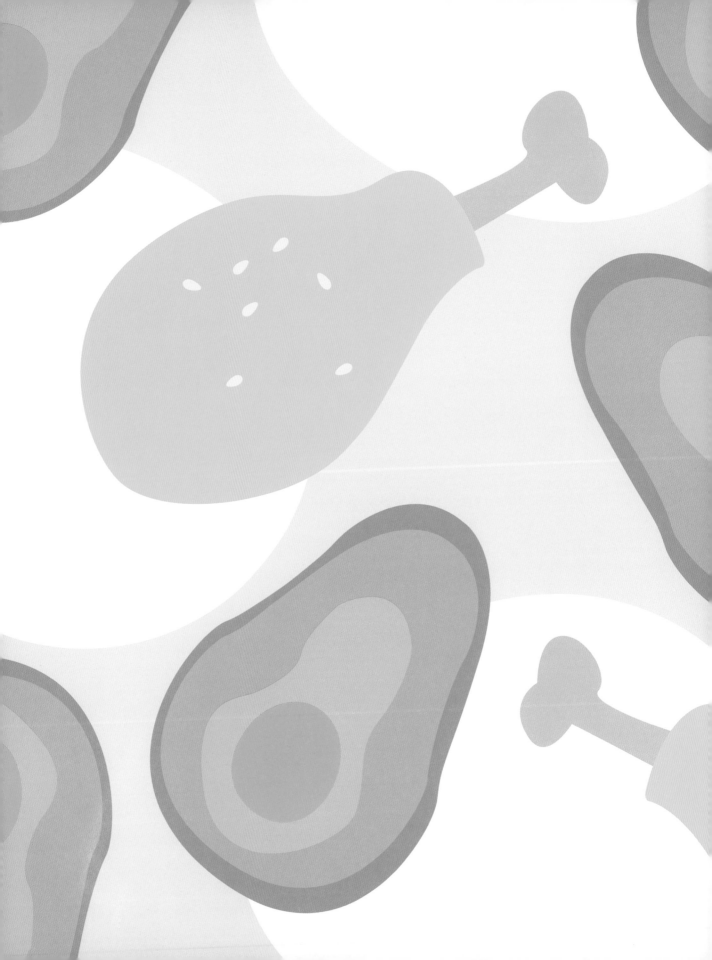

CHICKEN

Baked Quinoa-crumbed Chicken
WITH LIME AIOLI

SERVES 4–6   DF, GF, LC

My kids are obsessed with crumbed chicken so I decided to give it a healthy makeover. This recipe delivers all the crispiness, tenderness and deliciousness of crumbed chicken without the oily mess. Quinoa flakes are a great healthy option for crumbing because they are high in fibre, protein, vitamins and antioxidants. Every parent needs this recipe in their repertoire. I promise you'll be baking it weekly, just like I do.

40 g (⅓ cup) tapioca flour
2 eggs, whisked
150 g (1½ cups) quinoa flakes
35 g (⅓ cup) grated parmesan
2 teaspoons dried thyme
2 teaspoons sea salt flakes
¼ teaspoon ground white pepper
800 g (about 4) chicken breast fillets,
   each cut into 5–6 pieces
extra-virgin olive oil, for drizzling
lime wedges, to serve

LIME AIOLI
1 garlic clove, finely grated
1 egg yolk, at room temperature
1 teaspoon dijon mustard
1 tablespoon fresh lime juice
sea salt flakes and freshly ground black pepper
250 ml (1 cup) light olive oil

Preheat the oven to 220°C (fan-forced) and line a baking tray with baking paper or grease with olive oil.

Before you start crumbing your chicken, you need to set up three stations: tapioca flour in one bowl, whisked eggs in another, and the combined quinoa flakes, parmesan, thyme, salt and pepper on a tray.

Individually dip each piece of chicken in tapioca flour, dusting off the excess, then in the egg, and then firmly press into the quinoa mixture to coat on all sides.

Place the crumbed chicken on the prepared tray and drizzle with olive oil (or use oil spray if you prefer). Bake for 20 minutes or until golden and cooked through.

Meanwhile, to make the aioli, place the garlic, egg yolk, mustard, lime juice and a good pinch each of salt and pepper in a blender or food processor and blitz to combine. With the motor running, very slowly drizzle in the olive oil until the aioli starts to emulsify (see Tip). Taste and adjust the seasoning if necessary. The aioli can be stored in an airtight container in the fridge for up to a week.

Serve the chicken straight from the oven with the lime aioli and lime wedges for squeezing over.

TIP
- Emulsify means to combine two ingredients that do not ordinarily mix, like oil and water. For a smooth aioli, it's important to pour in the oil very slowly to disperse the droplets evenly.

Indian-spiced Chicken
& CAULIFLOWER TRAY BAKE

SERVES 4–6   DF, GF, LC

Traditionally, Indian-spiced chicken, like tandoori, is marinated in natural yoghurt but in my dairy-free version I use coconut yoghurt instead and it works a treat. This is a great midweek recipe to prep the night before so the flavours intensify, then you can simply throw it in the oven after work. Just 20 minutes later you will have the most aromatic Indian-spiced chicken that is low carb and gluten and dairy free. And the best part? Only one tray to clean!

150 g coconut yoghurt
2 tablespoons coconut oil
1 tablespoon finely grated ginger
4 garlic cloves, finely grated
2 teaspoons sea salt flakes
1 teaspoon ground cumin
1 teaspoon ground coriander
½ teaspoon ground turmeric
1 teaspoon garam masala
1 kg skinless chicken thigh fillets,
    fat trimmed, each cut into thirds
½ head of cauliflower, cut into florets
coriander leaves and lemon wedges, to serve

In a large bowl, mix together the yoghurt, coconut oil, ginger, garlic, salt, cumin, ground coriander, turmeric and garam masala. Add the chicken and cauliflower pieces and use your hands to coat well. Cover and marinate in the fridge for 1 hour or preferably overnight.

Preheat the oven to 200°C (fan-forced) and line a baking tray with baking paper.

Arrange the chicken and cauliflower in a single layer on the prepared tray. Bake for 20 minutes, tossing halfway through to ensure even colouring.

Scatter with coriander leaves and finish with a squeeze of lemon juice.

Sticky Miso-glazed CHICKEN WINGS

SERVES 4–6   DF, GF, LC

The beautiful umami notes in miso combined with honey creates the most glorious sweet and salty marinade for these sticky chicken wings. I use white miso for the marinade as it yields a slightly sweeter, mellower flavour than the darker varieties but if you have a soy allergy you could swap it out for a chickpea miso. So simple and quick to prepare, you could even marinate the wings the night before and throw them in the oven after work when your stomach is screaming MI-SO hungry!

1 kg chicken wings
1 tablespoon sesame seeds, to serve
2 tablespoons finely sliced spring onion,
   to serve

MISO MARINADE
2 tablespoons gluten-free white miso paste
2 tablespoons rice wine vinegar
1 tablespoon raw honey
1 teaspoon sesame oil
2 garlic cloves, finely grated
3 cm piece of ginger, finely grated

To make the marinade, combine the ingredients in a large bowl. Add the chicken wings and turn to coat well, then cover and marinate in the fridge for 30 minutes or preferably overnight.

Preheat the oven to 200°C (fan-forced) and line a baking tray with baking paper.

Arrange the chicken wings on the prepared tray in a single layer and bake for 40–45 minutes, turning and basting halfway through with any marinade left in the bowl to ensure the wings brown evenly.

Scatter with the sesame seeds and spring onion and serve.

TIP
+ This recipe also works well with chicken drumsticks.

Crispy Roast Chicken
& POTATOES IN A FLASH

SERVES 4–6 DF, GF

When you want roast chicken and potatoes quickly the best way to speed up the cooking time is to butterfly and flatten your chicken. Place a single layer of sliced potato underneath your beautifully seasoned chicken and as the chicken fat renders it will drip onto the potatoes, leaving you with the most delicious salty potato discs. It's like roast chicken with a side of crisps!

1 x 1.5 kg chicken, at room temperature
2 tablespoons extra-virgin olive oil
1 teaspoon dried oregano
1 teaspoon smoked paprika
1 teaspoon garlic powder
¼ teaspoon ground white pepper
sea salt flakes
5 waxy red potatoes, peeled and cut into
   1 cm-thick slices
lemon halves, to serve

Preheat the oven to 200°C (fan-forced) and line a shallow baking tray with baking paper.

Place the chicken on a board and pat dry with paper towel. Using sharp scissors, cut out the backbone. Flip the chicken over and press down on it firmly with the palm of your hand to flatten.

Brush 1 tablespoon of the olive oil all over the chicken. Combine the oregano, paprika, garlic powder, pepper and 1 tablespoon of salt flakes in a bowl. Sprinkle the spice mix over the chicken and evenly massage it into the skin.

Arrange the potato slices in a single layer on the prepared tray. Brush the potato with the remaining olive oil and sprinkle with salt.

Place a wire rack over the potato. Sit the chicken on the rack so the juices drip down and roast for 35–40 minutes until cooked through and crispy. Serve with lemon halves.

TIPS FOR CRISPY CHICKEN SKIN

- Moisture is the enemy of crispiness so it's important to pat the skin completely dry. If you have time, air-drying the chicken uncovered in the fridge overnight is even better.

- Sprinkle the skin liberally with sea salt flakes.

- Opt for garlic powder over crushed garlic to keep the seasoning dry.

- Crank up the heat and place the chicken on a rack to allow the hot air to circulate around the entire bird.

Chicken Curry
WITH PAPAYA & CORIANDER SALSA

SERVES 4–6   DF, GF

Quite often, curries made from scratch require a laundry list of obscure ingredients but not this one. Just blitz together a few pantry staples for an aromatic paste and let the chicken gently simmer away in the most sublime coconut curry sauce. The cooling salsa adds a welcome freshness and cuts through the richness of the sauce for the most spectacular flavour contrast.

1 kg skinless chicken thigh fillets, each cut into 2–3 pieces
1 tablespoon coconut oil
1 onion, diced
250 ml (1 cup) gluten-free chicken stock
270 ml coconut milk
1 tablespoon gluten-free tamari or coconut aminos
1 tablespoon fish sauce
juice of 1 lime, plus lime wedges to serve
1 teaspoon caster sugar
cooked jasmine rice (see page 21), to serve
coriander sprigs, to serve

CURRY PASTE
1 lemongrass stalk, white part only, bashed and finely sliced
3 garlic cloves, bashed
3 cm piece of ginger, finely grated
1 teaspoon ground cinnamon
1 teaspoon ground cumin
¼ teaspoon chilli powder
finely grated zest of 1 lime
3 tablespoons coconut oil, melted
1 tablespoon fish sauce

PAPAYA & CORIANDER SALSA
150 g papaya, finely chopped
½ red onion, finely diced
handful of coriander leaves, finely chopped
juice of 1 lime
1 teaspoon finely diced long red chilli (optional)

To make the curry paste, place the ingredients in a food processor and blitz to form a paste.

Combine the curry paste and chicken in a bowl, then cover and marinate in the fridge for at least an hour or preferably overnight.

Melt half of the coconut oil in a large saucepan over medium–high heat, add the chicken in batches and cook for 2–3 minutes on each side until nicely browned. Remove from the pan and set aside.

Add the remaining coconut oil to the pan, then add the onion and cook for a minute or so, stirring to release any caramelised bits caught on the base of the pan. Pour in the chicken stock and scrape the bottom of the pan again. Add the coconut milk, tamari or coconut aminos, fish sauce, lime juice and sugar and stir to combine. Return the chicken and any resting juices to the pan.

Simmer for 1 hour, uncovered, stirring occasionally. If the sauce is still a little thin, cook for another 5–10 minutes or until thickened.

Meanwhile, to make the salsa, combine the ingredients in a bowl.

Serve the chicken curry with rice and salsa. Scatter the coriander leaves over the top and serve with lime wedges on the side.

TIP
- In summer you can replace the papaya with tropical mango.

Chicken & Spinach Meatballs
IN A RICH TOMATO SAUCE

SERVES 4 DF, GF

My kids love anything small, playful and delicious, and these meatballs deliver on all three counts. The kids have no idea they are crammed with healthy greens, such as baby spinach and parsley, and I feel great knowing I've sneaked a few extra veggies onto the dinner plate. Meatballs are easy to freeze so you can double this recipe and freeze half to cook on a busy weeknight – just thaw to room temperature first.

1 tablespoon extra-virgin olive oil
cooked rice, pasta or quinoa (see page 21),
    to serve

CHICKEN & SPINACH MEATBALLS

500 g chicken mince
1 sebago potato (or another floury variety),
    peeled and very finely grated, excess
    moisture squeezed out
2 large handfuls of baby spinach leaves,
    finely chopped
3 tablespoons chopped flat-leaf parsley leaves
2 garlic cloves, finely grated
1 egg
finely grated zest of 1 small lemon
2 teaspoons ground cumin
generous pinch of sea salt flakes and freshly
    ground black pepper

RICH TOMATO SAUCE

1 tablespoon extra-virgin olive oil
1 onion, diced
400 ml tomato passata
125 ml (½ cup) gluten-free chicken stock
sea salt flakes and freshly ground black pepper

To make the meatballs, place all the ingredients in a bowl and mix well by hand. Refrigerate the mixture for 30 minutes to firm up, then roll it into about 16 meatballs. I find it helpful to wet or oil my hands prior to rolling to prevent the mince from sticking to my fingers.

Heat the olive oil in a large frying pan over medium–high heat. Sear the meatballs for 2–3 minutes, rotating them frequently until golden. Remove from the pan and set aside.

For the rich tomato sauce, heat the olive oil in the same pan and sauté the onion for 2–3 minutes until softened, stirring to release any caramelised bits caught on the base of the pan. Add the remaining ingredients, season with salt and pepper and stir to combine.

Return the meatballs to the pan and simmer, covered, for 20 minutes until the sauce has thickened and the meatballs are cooked through.

Serve with rice, pasta or quinoa to soak up the delicious sauce.

TIPS FOR PERFECT MEATBALLS

- Season generously with dried or fresh herbs and spices to add serious flavour.

- Add a starchy component like potato to keep them light and fluffy and don't roll them too tightly.

- Refrigerate your meatball mixture to intensify the flavour and firm it up, making the balls easier to roll.

One-tray
CHICKEN FAJITAS

SERVES 4–6 GF

Minimal washing up, maximum flavour – now that's my kinda midweek recipe. Just let your chicken strips and colourful veggies sizzle away in the oven for 30 minutes and you will be rewarded with the most vibrant and delicious Mexican fiesta. Fajitas are a great entertaining option when guests pop around unexpectedly because they are quick and simple to make and always a crowd pleaser.

6 skinless chicken thigh fillets, finely sliced
3 capsicums (various colours), deseeded and finely sliced
2 red onions, cut into thick slices
3 tablespoons extra-virgin olive oil
3 teaspoons sea salt flakes
2 teaspoons ground cumin
2 teaspoons smoked paprika
juice of 1 lime, plus lime wedges to serve
handful of coriander leaves, to serve
corn tortillas, to serve

OPTIONAL TOPPINGS
grated cheese of your choice
sliced avocado

Preheat the oven to 200°C (fan-forced) and line a large baking tray with baking paper.

Place the chicken, capsicum, onion, olive oil, salt, cumin and paprika on the prepared tray and combine with your hands. Spread the ingredients out in a single layer and bake for 30 minutes or until golden, tossing halfway through for even browning. Remove the tray from the oven, squeeze over the lime juice and scatter over the coriander.

Toast the tortillas over an open flame or in a dry frying pan or chargrill pan over high heat for a minute each side. Cover them with a tea towel to keep them warm and soft.

Fill the tortillas with the chicken fajita mixture and finish with your choice of toppings, if using. Serve with lime wedges on the side.

Chargrilled Za'atar Chicken
WITH PEA PUREE

SERVES 4–6   DF, GF, LC

Say goodbye to dry, boring chicken breast forever. These juicy za'atar fillets will make your tastebuds bellydance in just a matter of minutes. Pea puree sounds fancy but it's super simple to make – you'll be smearing your puree in no time for a lean, clean midweek dinner, plated like a pro. Your family will be so impressed.

3 x 200 g chicken breast fillets
500 g frozen peas
3 tablespoons extra-virgin olive oil
1 teaspoon sea salt flakes
za'atar, to serve

ZA'ATAR MARINADE
3 tablespoons extra-virgin olive oil
3 garlic cloves, finely grated
2 tablespoons za'atar
1 tablespoon sumac
3 teaspoons sea salt flakes

Cut each chicken breast in half horizontally. Place the fillets between two sheets of baking paper and gently pound with a rolling pin to flatten them a little (this will allow your chicken to cook faster and prevent it from drying out).

To make the za'atar marinade, combine all the ingredients in a glass or ceramic bowl. Add the chicken and massage to coat in the seasoning. Set aside to marinate for 30 minutes in the fridge or preferably overnight.

Cook the peas in a saucepan of salted boiling water for 3 minutes or until tender. Drain, reserving about 250 ml (1 cup) of the cooking water.

Transfer the warm peas to a food processor, add the olive oil, salt and 180 ml (¾ cup) of the reserved cooking water and blitz to a puree. Add more water if necessary to loosen it.

Heat a chargrill pan over medium–high heat. Working in batches, chargrill the chicken for 2 minutes on each side, then remove and set aside to rest for 2–3 minutes.

Smear the pea puree on a plate, top with the chicken and finish with a sprinkling of za'atar.

TIP
- For a super-smooth pea puree pass it through a sieve. You can replace the cooking water with gluten-free chicken stock for added depth of flavour.

PORK

Cochinita Pibil
(MEXICAN PULLED-PORK TACOS)

SERVES 6–8   DF, GF

Cochinita is the name given to traditional Mexican pulled pork cooked in a simple acidic mix of vinegar, garlic, onion and achiote – a vibrant spice with a distinct flavour unlike anything you have tasted before. The marinade is so easy to make and results in the most tender and insanely delicious pulled pork. My Mexican friend Tanya taught me this recipe so it does not get more authentic than this. Goodbye Tex-Mex, hello cochinita!

1 kg boneless pork leg or shoulder, cut into 5 cm chunks
20 gluten-free corn tortillas
¼ red cabbage, shredded
handful of coriander leaves
lime wedges, to serve

MARINADE
180 ml (¾ cup) white wine vinegar or apple cider vinegar
50 g achiote paste (see Tips)
1 onion, peeled and halved
1 garlic clove, roughly chopped
1 tablespoon sea salt flakes

PICKLED RED ONION
1 red onion, finely sliced
juice of 1 lime
pinch of sea salt flakes

To make the marinade, place the ingredients and 180 ml (¾ cup) of water in a food processor and blitz to form a smooth paste.

Place the pork in a large heavy-based saucepan and pour over the marinade. Cover and cook over low heat for 2½–3 hours or until the meat is very tender. Use two forks to shred the pork, then set aside and leave it to soak up all the liquid.

While the pork is cooking, prepare the pickled onion. Combine the ingredients in a bowl and set aside for 1 hour to pickle.

If you can, cook the tortillas directly over an open flame for maximum heat and crispy edges. Heat for about 10 seconds on each side. Otherwise, cook the tortillas in a dry frying pan or chargrill pan over high heat. Cover them with a tea towel to keep them warm and soft.

Fill the warm tortillas with cabbage, pulled pork, pickled onion and coriander. Serve with lime wedges.

TIPS
- Achiote paste is made from annatto seeds, spices and tomato and it has a unique earthy flavour. You can find it in gourmet grocers, Latin American supermarkets or online at Mexican food distributors.

- Cooking the pork in a pressure cooker will reduce your cooking time by two thirds. Just pour over the marinade, close the lid and cook on low for 1 hour.

Pork Youvetsi
(BRAISED PORK IN TOMATO SAUCE WITH ELBOW PASTA)

SERVES 4–6 GF

Youvetsi is a comforting winter stew traditionally made with risoni but in my gluten-free version I have swapped it out for baby elbow pasta. This warming tomato-based dish is very popular with kids – they love scooping out the pasta from the bottom of the bowl. If you prefer you can use chicken, beef or lamb instead of pork, and different pasta shapes as long as they are small.

1 kg boneless pork shoulder, cut into
   4 cm chunks
sea salt flakes and freshly ground black pepper
3 tablespoons extra-virgin olive oil
2 large onions, diced
2 garlic cloves, finely grated
2 dried bay leaves
2 tablespoons tomato paste
125 ml (½ cup) red wine
400 g can crushed tomatoes
1 cinnamon stick
pinch of grated nutmeg
200 g gluten-free elbow pasta
grated kefalograviera or parmesan, to serve

Preheat the oven to 180°C (fan-forced).

Season the pork with salt and pepper. Heat half the olive oil in a large flameproof casserole dish over medium–high heat, add the pork in batches and brown on all sides for about 5 minutes. Remove and set aside.

Heat the remaining oil in the dish and sauté the onion for 2–3 minutes. Add the garlic, bay leaves and tomato paste and cook for another 30 seconds. Deglaze the pan with the red wine, stirring to release any caramelised bits caught on the base, and simmer for 2–3 minutes or until reduced by half.

Return the pork and any resting juices to the dish and add the crushed tomatoes, cinnamon, nutmeg and 1.25 litres of water. Season with an extra pinch of salt, then cover and braise in the oven for 2 hours.

Remove the dish from the oven and stir in the pasta. Put the lid back on and bake for another 15 minutes or until the pasta is al dente. Finish with grated kefalograviera or parmesan and a grinding of pepper and serve.

TIP
- Instead of kefalograviera or parmesan you could crumble over Greek feta just before serving – it's just as delicious!

Pork Fricassee
(BRAISED PORK WITH CELERY, LEEK & DILL)

SERVES 4–6 DF, GF, LC

Celery and leek play a starring role in this slow-cooked Greek stew. The braised pork gently simmers away in a pool of greens and at the final stage the stew is brought to life by the zesty avgolemono sauce. You can swap out leek for your favourite greens, such as silverbeet, and don't forget to mop up that beautiful sauce with some crusty gluten-free bread (see page 29).

1 kg boneless pork shoulder or neck, cut into 5 cm chunks
sea salt flakes and freshly ground black pepper
3 tablespoons extra-virgin olive oil
1 onion, sliced
2 celery stalks, sliced
1 leek, white and light green part, sliced
125 ml (½ cup) white wine
2 tablespoons chopped dill fronds, plus extra to serve
2 tablespoons chopped flat-leaf parsley leaves, plus extra leaves to serve

AVGOLEMONO (LEMON–EGG SAUCE)

2 eggs, at room temperature
juice of 1 large lemon

Preheat the oven to 180°C (fan-forced).

Season the pork with salt and pepper. Heat half the olive oil in a large flameproof casserole dish over medium–high heat, add the pork in batches and brown on all sides for about 5 minutes. Remove and set aside.

Heat the remaining oil in the dish, add the onion, celery, leek and a pinch of salt and sauté for 5 minutes or until softened. Deglaze the pan with the white wine, stirring to release any caramelised bits caught on the base of the dish, and simmer for 2–3 minutes or until reduced by half.

Return the pork and any resting juices to the dish and pour in 1 litre of water. Cover and braise in the oven for 2 hours. Remove the dish from the oven and stir in the dill.

To make the avgolemono, whisk the eggs in a medium bowl, then pour in the lemon juice and whisk to combine. Slowly pour in a few ladles of the warm braising liquid and whisk vigorously to combine, then pour it back into the braise and gently stir it in.

Garnish with parsley and dill fronds and serve.

TIP

- Make sure you cut the pork into fairly large chunks because it will shrink in the oven.

Sticky Pork Ribs
WITH TAMARI, HONEY & MUSTARD GLAZE

SERVES 4–6   DF, GF, LC

Sticky. Jammy. Salty. Sweet. Need I say more? This is a minimum input, maximum output recipe.
Just mix equal amounts of tamari, honey and mustard with a few spices and your work is basically done.
Marinating overnight intensifies the flavours, resulting in succulent, tender pork with an explosive flavour
punch. My kids love the primal ritual of gnawing meat off the bones, and the messy, sticky fingers
are totally worth it!

3 tablespoons gluten-free wholegrain mustard
3 tablespoons gluten-free tamari or
  coconut aminos
3 tablespoons raw honey
3 garlic cloves, finely grated
1 tablespoon finely grated ginger
1 bird's eye chilli, deseeded and finely
  chopped (optional)
2 x 800 g racks American pork ribs
375 ml (1½ cups) dry sherry

Whisk together the mustard, tamari or coconut aminos, honey, garlic, ginger and chilli (if using) to make a marinade. Place the ribs in a roasting tin and rub the marinade all over on both sides. Set aside to marinate in the fridge for 1 hour (or overnight if time permits).

Preheat the oven to 160°C (fan-forced).

Pour the sherry into the tin, cover very tightly with a sheet of baking paper and then foil, and bake for 2 hours.

Remove the paper and foil and increase the temperature to 200°C (fan-forced). Baste the ribs with the pan juices and bake for a further 10–15 minutes, basting every 5 minutes, to reduce the sauce and achieve a caramelised sticky glaze on the pork.

TIP
- Placing a sheet of baking paper between the foil and the meat prevents the meat from sticking to the foil and creates an extra layer of insulation to trap the steam.

- If the pork is still not caramelised at the end of cooking, you can place it under a hot grill for 5 minutes to crisp up.

Pork Yeeros
WITH GLUTEN-FREE PITA BREAD

SERVES 4   GF

I grew up on yeeros (also called gyros or souva). It was a staple at every Greek barbecue as a kid and my late-night street-food fix as a young adult. Trendy interpretations run the spectrum from seafood to mustard mayo but nothing beats the traditional version filled with succulent pork, creamy tzatziki, juicy tomato, onion slivers and chips … hand cut of course! The homemade gluten-free pita bread is so easy to make – light and crispy, you never have to miss out on classic pita again.

400 g pork neck, cut into 3 cm cubes
juice of 1 lemon (optional)
4 Gluten-free Pita Breads (page 30)
1 tomato, halved and sliced
1 small red onion, finely sliced
Chunky Greek Oven Fries (page 110)

MARINADE

3 tablespoons extra-virgin olive oil
juice of ½ lemon
2 garlic cloves, finely grated
1 tablespoon sea salt flakes
2 teaspoons thyme leaves or dried oregano
1 teaspoon dijon mustard
⅛ teaspoon ground white pepper

TZATZIKI

1 Lebanese cucumber, halved lengthways
    and deseeded
1 teaspoon sea salt flakes
300 g Greek yoghurt (or coconut yoghurt
    for a dairy-free version)
1 garlic clove, finely grated
1 tablespoon white wine vinegar
1 tablespoon extra-virgin olive oil
1 tablespoon finely chopped dill fronds

To make the marinade, combine the ingredients in a glass or ceramic bowl. Add the pork and mix until well coated. Marinate in the fridge for a few hours, or overnight if time permits.

Soak four bamboo skewers in water for 20 minutes or so to prevent them from burning during cooking.

Meanwhile, to make the tzatziki, grate the cucumber and sprinkle with the salt. Sit for 10 minutes, then firmly squeeze out any excess moisture and add the cucumber to a bowl with the remaining ingredients. Stir to combine.

Thread the pork pieces evenly onto the skewers.

Heat a chargrill pan over high heat until smoking hot. Cook the pork skewers for 5 minutes, turning until browned all over and cooked through. Remove from the pan and set aside to rest. You can squeeze over a little lemon juice, if desired.

Smear a dollop of tzatziki on each pita bread, top with the pork skewers, tomato, onion and chips and roll up to serve. Don't forget to pull out the skewers!

TIPS

- Purchase a good-quality thick, creamy Greek yoghurt for the tzatziki. If your yoghurt is runny, suspend it in a piece of muslin or cheesecloth over a bowl for a few hours to drain off the water and give a thicker consistency.

- I prefer to leave the skin on my cucumber for added texture in my tzatziki but feel free to peel it if you prefer.

- The pork can be swapped out for chicken, lamb or beef.

- Any leftover tzatziki can be stored in the fridge in an airtight container for up to 1 week.

School Bell
SAN CHOY BOW

SERVES 4–6   DF, GF, LC

This is the dish my kids request most frequently after school. They love the playfulness of filling crisp lettuce cups with steaming hot pork and veggies, and given all that healthy goodness I am happy to oblige. You can easily swap out the pork for other proteins, such as minced chicken or shredded duck. I find fattier cuts of meat work best to keep the filling moist, but mushrooms are a beautiful vegetarian option, too.

2 tablespoons peanut oil
1 onion, finely sliced
1 garlic clove, finely grated
1 tablespoon finely grated ginger
500 g fatty pork mince
1 teaspoon caster sugar
2 tablespoons gluten-free tamari or
   coconut aminos
1 tablespoon gluten-free oyster sauce
½ teaspoon sesame oil
1 large carrot, julienned
100 g (1 cup) mung bean sprouts
3 tablespoons finely sliced spring onion
iceberg lettuce leaves, to serve
chopped roasted peanuts, for
   sprinkling (optional)

Heat the peanut oil in a wok over high heat. Add the onion, garlic and ginger and stir-fry for 1 minute.

Add the pork in batches and let it sear for a minute to form a crust, then break it up with a wooden spoon. Sprinkle over the sugar and cook for another minute to start browning the pork.

Pour in the tamari or coconut aminos, oyster sauce and sesame oil and cook for 1 minute. Add the carrot, bean sprouts and spring onion and toss to combine, then remove from the heat once the pork is cooked through.

Spoon the filling into the lettuce cups and sprinkle with chopped peanuts, if using.

Crispy Pork Belly
WITH BRAISED FENNEL & CARROT

SERVES 4–6   DF, GF, LC

Fantastically crunchy crackling and incredibly tender meat are two must haves when it comes to pork belly. I find I get the best results by roasting the pork skin-side down at a low temperature to slowly render the fat, then turning it skin-side up and blasting it with high heat at the final stage. The braised fennel and carrot soak up all the beautiful pan juices and the lemon and aniseed deliver the knockout punch.

1 tablespoon extra-virgin olive oil
1.5 kg pork belly, skin scored at 1 cm intervals and patted dry
1 tablespoon sea salt flakes, plus extra for sprinkling
500 ml (2 cups) gluten-free chicken stock
2 fennel bulbs, cut into 1 cm-thick slices
2 large carrots, halved lengthways, then quartered
1 lemon, cut into 1 cm-thick slices
2 garlic cloves, finely sliced
3 star anise
freshly ground black pepper

Preheat the oven to 180°C (fan-forced).

Drizzle the olive oil over the pork skin and sprinkle with salt, then firmly massage the seasoning into the skin.

Place the pork belly skin-side down in a 35 cm × 30 cm baking tray – you want it to fit snugly. Roast for 1½ hours.

Take the tin out of the oven and increase the heat to 220°C (fan-forced). Remove the pork from the tin, then pour in the chicken stock and scrape up any caramelised bits caught on the base of the tin. Arrange the fennel, carrot, lemon, garlic and star anise in the tin in a single layer and season with pepper. Place the pork on top skin-side up, taking care to keep the skin dry.

Roast the pork for a further 30 minutes or until the skin crackles and the vegetables are tender. If your crackling is not quite crisp enough, just blast it under the grill for 5 minutes. Sprinkle some more salt flakes over before serving.

TIP

- For super-crispy crackling, refrigerate the pork belly uncovered overnight (or for at least 3 hours) to really dry out the skin. Moisture is the enemy of crispy skin.

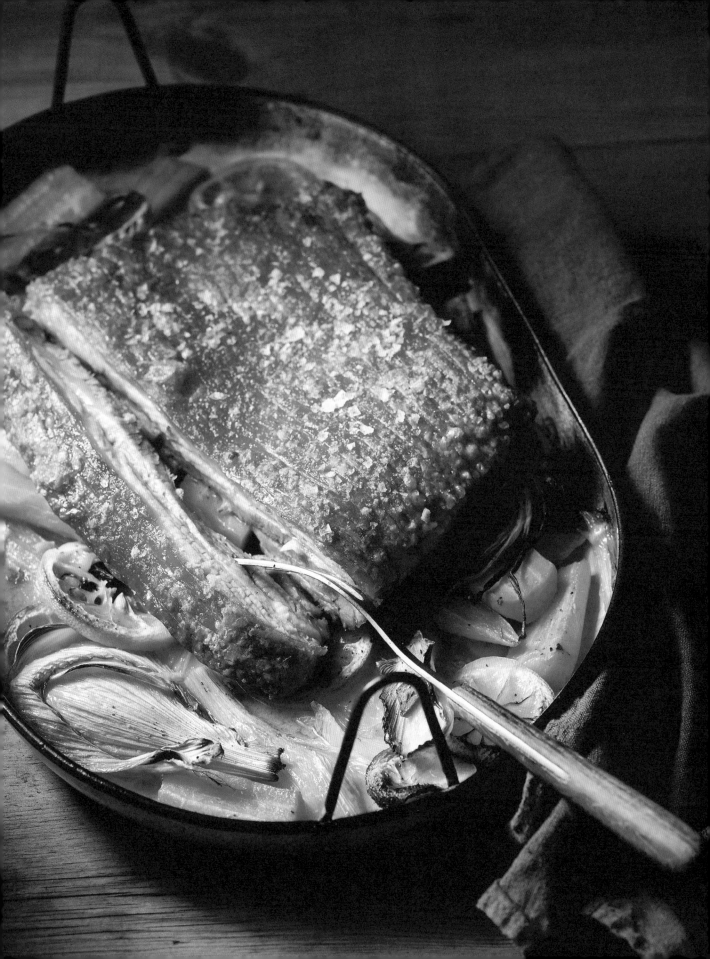

Easy One-pot
CARAMELISED PORK

SERVES 6 DF, GF

I love an easy recipe where you can throw everything in a pot and walk away. This tender, caramelised pork falls apart when it hits the fork without adding sugar or fat to the recipe. The sweetness comes from fresh coconut water, while the acidic lime juice tenderises the meat. The pork then magically fries in its own fat at the final stage, producing crispy, caramelised chunks of heaven. The perfect one-pot family meal.

1 tablespoon ground cumin
1 teaspoon garlic powder
1 tablespoon sea salt flakes
2 teaspoons ground coriander
1 teaspoon ground white pepper
1.2 kg boneless pork shoulder or neck,
    cut into 5 cm cubes
500 ml (2 cups) fresh coconut water
    (from about 1 young coconut) or
    packaged coconut water
125 ml (½ cup) fresh lime juice
cooked white rice (see page 21), to serve
lime wedges, to serve
coriander sprigs, to serve

Combine the dried spices in a bowl and rub all over the pork. Cover and marinate for at least 30 minutes or in the fridge overnight.

Place the seasoned pork in a large heavy-based saucepan and pour in the coconut water, lime juice and 250 ml (1 cup) of water. Bring to the boil over high heat, then reduce the heat to low and simmer, covered, for 1½ hours.

Remove the lid and simmer uncovered for another hour.

Keep your eye on the pork at the end of the cooking time because the liquid will evaporate quickly and the pork will fry in its own fat. When it reaches this stage, gently turn the pork cubes to brown on all sides. Serve with steamed rice, lime wedges and coriander sprigs scattered over the top.

TIP
- For a low-carb meal, replace the rice with cauliflower rice.

Toasted Spice
PORK RIBS

SERVES 4–6 DF, GF, LC

Toasting spices releases their aromatic oils and intensifies their flavour, adding a greater complexity to your dishes. I often prepare a larger batch of the fennel spice rub in advance and store it in an airtight container for up to four months. It makes this such an easy dish to throw together when I'm short of time. Pork and fennel are a match made in heaven – the aniseed notes in the salty spice rub cut through the fatty pork and create a beautiful crispy crust under the hot grill.

2 teaspoons fennel seeds
1 teaspoon coriander seeds
¼ teaspoon white peppercorns
1½ tablespoons sea salt flakes
1 teaspoon garlic powder
10 x 140 g pork spare ribs

Place the fennel seeds, coriander seeds and white peppercorns in a small dry frying pan and toast over low heat for 2–3 minutes until you smell their aroma. Keep an eye on them and toss frequently as they can burn easily. Transfer the spices to a mortar, add the salt and garlic powder and grind with a pestle.

Place the pork on a baking tray lined with baking paper, and massage the spice rub all over the ribs. Marinate uncovered for 30 minutes or overnight in the fridge to intensify the flavours and remove moisture.

Transfer the ribs to your oven grill tray. Grill for 10–12 minutes on each side until the pork is golden and crispy.

LAMB

Slow-cooked Lamb Shoulder
WITH LEMON POTATOES

SERVES 6–8   DF, GF

Fall-apart lamb nestled in a bed of lemony potatoes is what Sunday roast looks like at my place.
This recipe is ridiculously easy – just keep the roasting tin sealed very tightly and you are guaranteed
juicy, melt-in-your-mouth meat bathed in a light lemony sauce. Shoulder is my preferred cut of lamb
for slow cooking because the collagen and fat slowly melt away in the oven, resulting in richly
flavoured, tender meat.

1 × 2.5 kg lamb shoulder, bone in (see Note)
5 garlic cloves, sliced
3 tablespoons extra-virgin olive oil
2 rosemary sprigs, leaves picked and
  roughly chopped
1 tablespoon dried oregano
2 tablespoons sea salt flakes
pinch of freshly ground black pepper
500 ml (2 cups) gluten-free chicken stock
juice of 1 large lemon, plus extra wedges
  to serve
6 desiree potatoes (or another waxy variety),
  peeled and cut into thick wedges

Preheat the oven to 160°C (fan-forced).

Place the lamb in a roasting tin. Make incisions all over the lamb
with a small sharp knife and fill with the garlic slices. Drizzle over the
olive oil and season with the rosemary, oregano, salt and pepper, then
firmly massage the seasoning into the lamb.

Pour the chicken stock into the tin and squeeze in the lemon juice.
Cover the tin very tightly with a sheet of baking paper, then foil and
roast for 3 hours.

Remove the tin from the oven and baste the lamb with the pan juices.
Add the potato wedges and season with a sprinkling of salt, then
cover tightly and return to the oven for 1 hour.

Increase the temperature to 200°C (fan-forced). Remove the
paper and foil and baste the lamb with the pan juices, then roast,
uncovered, for another 20 minutes or until the lamb is golden brown.

Adjust the seasoning to taste and serve the lamb and potatoes with
the pan juices and lemon wedges.

NOTE
- This might seem like a lot of lamb, but once you factor in the bone it's
  only about 1.8 kg of meat.

Lamb Kleftiko
(BRAISED LAMB WITH POTATO & STRETCHY CHEESE)

SERVES 4–6   GF

Lamb kleftiko is my go-to meal when entertaining for several reasons: most of the work can be done in advance, it's easy to make, great for sharing and, most importantly, it's crammed with spectacular flavour. The tender lamb is deliciously succulent and it's accompanied by irresistible nuggets of hot, stretchy cheese and potato swimming in a zesty stock. I don't think I've ever had guests leave without requesting the recipe.

1 × 1 kg deboned lamb shoulder, cut into large chunks
sea salt flakes and freshly ground black pepper
2 tablespoons extra-virgin olive oil
1 large onion, diced
4 garlic cloves, sliced
1 tablespoon finely chopped rosemary leaves
1 tablespoon finely chopped thyme leaves
750 ml (3 cups) gluten-free chicken stock
2 large waxy potatoes (such as desiree or pontiac), peeled and cut into 3 cm cubes
2 large tomatoes, cut into 3 cm cubes
150 g kefalotyri or kefalograviera cheese (see Tip), cut into 3 cm cubes
juice of 1 lemon

Preheat the oven to 160°C (fan-forced).

Season the lamb with salt and pepper. Heat the olive oil in a large flameproof casserole dish over medium–high heat and brown the lamb for 5 minutes on all sides. Remove from the dish and set aside.

Add the onion and sauté for 2–3 minutes until softened. Add the garlic, rosemary and thyme and sauté for another 30 seconds.

Return the lamb and any resting juices to the dish and pour in the chicken stock. Cover and braise in the oven for 1½ hours.

Remove the dish from the oven and stir in the potato, tomato, cheese and lemon juice. Bake, covered, for 1 hour or until the potato is tender. Season to taste with salt and pepper and serve.

TIP

- Kefalograviera and kefalotyri are hard white sheep's milk cheeses that hold their shape when cooked. You can find them in European delis and gourmet grocers. If unavailable, use Greek feta instead.

Tuesday Night
LAMB CUTLETS

SERVES 4   DF, GF, LC

Meat-free Monday is usually followed by red-meat Tuesday at our place, and lamb cutlets feature regularly because they are quick, easy and delicious. I always ask my butcher to french and bash my cutlets. The flatter surface area makes them super crispy when they hit the hot pan and trimming the fat makes it easier for the kids to eat them off the bone.

12 lamb cutlets, frenched and bashed
3 teaspoons extra-virgin olive oil
2 teaspoons dried oregano
2 garlic cloves, finely grated
1 tablespoon sea salt flakes
¼ teaspoon ground white pepper
lemon wedges, to serve

Place the lamb cutlets in a bowl or on a baking tray. Add the olive oil, oregano, garlic, salt and pepper and massage firmly into the cutlets.

Heat a cast-iron chargrill pan over high heat. Add the cutlets and cook for 3–4 minutes on each side until charred and crispy. Remove and rest for 5 minutes, then serve with a squeeze of lemon juice.

TIP

- Drizzling the olive oil over the cutlets instead of the pan prevents the pan from smoking too much.

The Only Moussaka Recipe
YOU WILL EVER NEED

SERVES 6–8 GF

Moussaka is the national dish of my parents' homeland, the quintessential Hellenic meal. For me moussaka must meet two strict criteria: it must not be too heavy or greasy, and it must be lamb in the bolognese, not beef! To keep my moussaka light I steam my potato slices instead of frying them; they soak up the rich bolognese beautifully and perfectly balance the crispy eggplant and velvety bechamel. It may sound like a big call, but after one bite you will immediately understand why this is the only moussaka recipe you will ever need. Kali Orexi!

2 large eggplants, finely sliced
sea salt flakes
extra-virgin olive oil, for pan-frying
2 large sebago potatoes (or another floury
    variety), peeled, finely sliced and steamed
    until cooked (see Tips)
grated kefalograviera cheese, to finish

LAMB BOLOGNESE
3 tablespoons extra-virgin olive oil
1 onion, finely diced
2 garlic cloves, roughly chopped
500 g lamb mince
2 tablespoons tomato paste
600 g canned crushed tomatoes
1 teaspoon dried oregano
1 tablespoon chopped rosemary leaves
1 cinnamon stick
generous pinch of grated nutmeg
sea salt flakes and freshly ground black pepper

BECHAMEL
100 g butter
100 g (¾ cup) gluten-free plain flour
800 ml full-cream milk
100 g kefalograviera cheese, grated
pinch of ground cinnamon
1 egg, whisked
sea salt flakes and freshly ground black pepper

For the lamb bolognese, heat the olive oil in a large saucepan over medium heat, add the onion and sauté for 2–3 minutes until softened. Add the garlic and sauté for another 30 seconds.

Add the mince in chunks and let it sear for a minute to form a crust, then break it up with a wooden spoon. Stir in the tomato paste and cook for another minute. Add the tomatoes, oregano, rosemary, cinnamon and nutmeg, and season with salt and pepper. Cover and simmer over low heat for 1 hour, then taste and adjust the seasoning if necessary.

While the bolognese is simmering, salt the eggplant slices. Drizzle olive oil into a frying pan set over medium–high heat and pan-fry the eggplant in batches until golden on both sides. Drain on paper towel.

To make the bechamel, melt the butter in a saucepan over low heat. Whisk in the flour to form a smooth paste and continue whisking for another 30 seconds to cook off the flour. While still whisking, slowly pour in the milk until a thick sauce is achieved. Add the cheese and cinnamon and stir until melted and smooth. Remove the pan from the heat and whisk in the egg. Season to taste.

Preheat the oven to 200°C (fan-forced).

To assemble the moussaka, oil a large 40 cm × 28 cm baking dish. Lay the eggplant on the base and top with the lamb bolognese. Arrange the potato slices over the lamb and cover with the bechamel. Grate a little kefalograveria over the top, then bake for 45 minutes or until golden. Remove from the oven and let it rest for 10 minutes before slicing and serving.

TIPS
- The potato slices can be steamed in the microwave or in a steamer basket on the stovetop.

- You can assemble your moussaka a day ahead and bake the next day, or freeze it uncooked for up to a month. You can cook it straight from the freezer – just add another 20 minutes or so to the baking time.

Moroccan Lamb Tajine
WITH PUMPKIN & QUINOA

SERVES 4–6 DF, GF

This aromatic tajine is so easy to make – you simply throw everything in a pot and let it simmer away. You get subtle sweetness from cinnamon-scented pumpkin, freshness from fragrant herbs and juiciness from succulent fall-apart lamb. Traditionally, tajines are served with couscous but in my gluten-free version I suggest quinoa, which is far superior nutritionally. Kids love the fluffy texture and nutty taste of quinoa and it soaks up the sauce beautifully in this family recipe.

1 × 1 kg deboned lamb shoulder, trimmed of fat
   and cut into 5 cm chunks
extra-virgin olive oil, for pan-frying
500 ml (2 cups) gluten-free chicken stock
juice of 1 lemon
300 g peeled butternut pumpkin,
   cut into 3 cm cubes
coriander leaves, to serve
cooked quinoa (see page 21), to serve

MARINADE
3 garlic cloves, roughly chopped
2 cm piece of ginger, roughly chopped
1 small onion, halved
small handful of coriander leaves
½ teaspoon ground coriander
½ teaspoon ground cumin
½ teaspoon ground cinnamon
3 tablespoons extra-virgin olive oil
1 tablespoon sea salt flakes
pinch of freshly ground black pepper

To make the marinade, place the ingredients in a food processor and blitz to form a paste. Pour into a glass or ceramic bowl, add the lamb and turn to coat well. Cover and marinate in the fridge for at least 3 hours or overnight.

Preheat the oven to 180°C (fan-forced).

Heat a drizzle of olive oil in a tajine or flameproof casserole dish over medium–high heat and sear the lamb for 5 minutes or until browned all over.

Pour in the chicken stock and lemon juice, then cover and place in the oven for 2 hours. Remove the dish from the oven and stir in the pumpkin, then bake for another 30 minutes.

Remove the tajine from the oven and adjust the seasoning if necessary. Scatter with coriander leaves and serve with quinoa.

Lamb Koftas
WITH MINT YOGHURT

SERVES 6 GF

Middle Eastern koftas are a great way to get kids excited about cooking. My kids love throwing all the aromatic herbs and spices into a bowl and moulding the mince mixture onto the skewers. The koftas pack a flavour punch and the creamy mint yoghurt perfectly cuts through the richness of the spiced lamb. Koftas are delicious stuffed in pita bread with extra herbs but you can also enjoy them with rice.

extra-virgin olive oil, for brushing
juice of 1 lemon
handful of flat-leaf parsley
finely sliced red onion, to serve
Gluten-free Pita Breads (page 30), to serve

KOFTAS
600 g lamb mince
1 small red onion, grated, excess moisture
    squeezed out
2 garlic cloves, finely grated
3 teaspoons sea salt flakes
2 teaspoons ground cumin
1 teaspoon sumac
pinch of freshly ground black pepper
3 tablespoons finely chopped flat-leaf
    parsley leaves
3 tablespoons finely chopped mint leaves

MINT YOGHURT
2 tablespoons chopped mint leaves
1 garlic clove, roughly chopped
pinch of sea salt flakes
250 g (1 cup) Greek yoghurt (or coconut
    yoghurt for a dairy-free version)
1 tablespoon lemon juice

To make the koftas, place the ingredients in a bowl and mix together well. Rest in the fridge for 30 minutes, then dampen your hands and mould the mixture evenly onto 12 flat wooden or metal skewers in a long flat shape. If using wooden skewers, soak them in cold water for 30 minutes before using.

Heat a large chargrill pan over high heat. Brush the koftas with olive oil and cook for 5 minutes or until charred and cooked through, turning halfway. Squeeze over the lemon juice and set aside to rest for 2–3 minutes.

To make the mint yoghurt, place the mint, garlic and salt in a mortar and grind to a paste with the pestle. Add the yoghurt and lemon juice and stir to combine.

Serve the koftas with the mint yoghurt, parsley, onion and pita breads.

TIP
- If using wooden skewers, soak them in water first to prevent them from burning.

One-pan Lamb Chops
WITH MUSTARD-THYME SAUCE

SERVES 4   DF, GF, LC

Simple one-pan recipes are a lifesaver during the week. Crisp on the outside and juicy in the middle, these economical lamb chops only take 10 minutes to cook, and your family will love the creamy mustard sauce made without a single drop of cream or butter! This recipe is super versatile, so feel free to swap the lamb for pork and play with different herbs if you like. File this midweek saviour under quick, easy and yummy!

8 lamb chops, fat removed
2 garlic cloves, finely grated
1 tablespoon chopped thyme leaves, plus extra
   to serve
2 teaspoons sea salt flakes
pinch of freshly ground black pepper
2 tablespoons extra-virgin olive oil

MUSTARD-THYME SAUCE
1 tablespoon extra-virgin olive oil
1 golden shallot, finely chopped
1 garlic clove, finely grated
180 ml (¾ cup) white wine
2 tablespoons dijon mustard
1 tablespoon thyme leaves
sea salt flakes and freshly ground black pepper

Place the lamb chops on a baking tray. Add the garlic, thyme, salt and pepper and drizzle over 1 tablespoon of the olive oil, then massage the seasoning into the lamb. Set aside to marinate for 30 minutes or in the fridge overnight.

Heat the remaining olive oil in a large frying pan over high heat. Add the lamb chops fat-side down first by firmly placing them in the pan sideways. Sear the fat for 3 minutes until it crisps up, then lay the chops flat and cook for 2 minutes on each side. Remove from the pan and set aside.

To make the mustard–thyme sauce, reduce the heat to low and heat the olive oil in the pan. Add the shallot and garlic and sauté for 30 seconds. Pour in the wine and stir to release any caramelised bits caught on the base of the pan, then simmer until reduced by half. Add the mustard and thyme and simmer for a minute or two until slightly thickened. Season to taste with salt and pepper.

Return the chops to the pan and turn to coat in the sauce, then serve, spooning any remaining sauce over the top and sprinkling over the extra thyme leaves.

Lamb Shanks
WITH POMEGRANATE-BALSAMIC GLAZE

SERVES 4–6   DF, GF

Fall-apart braised lamb shanks are always a crowd pleaser and this spiced sticky glaze takes them to the next level. You get tartness and subtle sweetness from the pomegranate, acidic zing and a richness from the balsamic vinegar, and fragrant notes from the rosemary, allspice and cinnamon. Glossy and complex with spectacular flavour, this restaurant-quality dish is so easy to prepare at home.

4–6 large lamb shanks, fat trimmed
sea salt flakes and freshly ground black pepper
80 ml (⅓ cup) extra-virgin olive oil
1 large onion, sliced
2 tablespoons chopped rosemary leaves
4 garlic cloves, sliced
500 ml (2 cups) pomegranate juice
3 tablespoons balsamic vinegar
1 teaspoon ground allspice
1 cinnamon stick
pomegranate seeds and small mint leaves, to serve
cooked quinoa (see page 21), to serve

Preheat the oven to 150°C (fan-forced).

Season the lamb generously with salt and pepper. Heat 2 tablespoons of the olive oil in a large flameproof casserole dish over medium–high heat and sear the lamb shanks for 8 minutes, turning regularly to brown all over. Remove from the dish and set aside.

Reduce the heat to low. Add the remaining olive oil, then the onion and rosemary and sauté for 2–3 minutes until softened. Add the garlic and sauté for 30 seconds. Pour in the pomegranate juice and balsamic vinegar and stir to release any caramelised bits caught on the base of the dish, then add the allspice, cinnamon and an extra pinch of salt and pepper.

Bring to a simmer, then cover and braise in the oven for 2–2½ hours until the lamb is fork tender. Remove the shanks and set aside. Place the dish on the stovetop and simmer uncovered for 5 minutes or until the glaze has reduced to your desired thickness. Take off the heat and return the shanks to the dish, turning to coat in the glaze.

Divide the lamb shanks among plates and garnish with pomegranate seeds and mint leaves. Serve with quinoa.

VARIATION
- Replace the quinoa with creamy potato mash.

BEEF

Steak
WITH CHIMICHURRI SAUCE

SERVES 4   DF, GF, LC

Chimichurri is my all-time favourite steak sauce. I love the punchy combination of fresh herbs and red wine vinegar. For a more intense flavour I marinate the meat in chimichurri before cooking it, and then serve it as an accompaniment when the steaks are ready. Chimichurri is a 'clean' sauce because it's gluten, dairy and sugar free and packed with antioxidants from the vibrant greens and garlic. The chilli is optional; I tend to leave it out for the kids but if you love heat then fire it up!

---

4 x 200 g steaks of your choice (such as
scotch fillet, sirloin or eye fillet)
sea salt flakes

CHIMICHURRI
3 garlic cloves, roughly chopped
2 teaspoons sea salt flakes, plus extra if needed
1 teaspoon ground cumin
pinch of freshly ground black pepper
180 ml (¾ cup) extra-virgin olive oil
80 ml (⅓ cup) red wine vinegar, plus extra
if needed
handful of flat-leaf parsley leaves,
finely chopped
handful of coriander leaves, finely chopped
1 bird's eye chilli, deseeded and finely chopped
(optional)

To make the chimichurri, place the garlic, salt, cumin and pepper in a mortar and pound with a pestle. Stir through the remaining ingredients and adjust the seasoning as required with more salt or vinegar.

Marinate the steaks in one-third of the sauce for 30 minutes or in the fridge overnight.

Bring the steaks to room temperature and season with salt.

Heat a chargrill pan over high heat. Add the steaks in batches and cook for 3 minutes on each side for medium–rare or 4 minutes for medium.

Remove the steaks from the pan and rest on a wire rack for half the cooking time.

Serve with the remaining chimichurri sauce.

TIPS
Four rules for perfect steak:

1 Bring the steak to room temperature before grilling to ensure even cooking.

2 Ensure your chargrill pan is hot enough to seal the surface and form a crispy crust.

3 Rest the steak after cooking to relax the muscle fibres and allow the juices to run back into the meat.

4 Slice against the grain to shorten the muscle fibres and make the steak easier to chew.

Kokkinisto Beef

SERVES 4–6   DF, GF

Kokkino means red in Greek. Here it is a reference to the simmering tomato sauce scented with cinnamon, cloves and thyme that slowly cooks the beef. I have many childhood memories of a comforting plate of kokkinisto on a rainy day– it's one of those traditional dishes you'll find in every Greek household. This recipe also works beautifully with chicken thighs, and the rice can be swapped out for pasta sprinkled with grated kefalograviera cheese.

1 kg blade or chuck beef, cut into 5 cm chunks
sea salt flakes and freshly ground black pepper
80 ml (⅓ cup) extra-virgin olive oil
1 large onion, chopped
2 celery stalks, cut into thick slices
1 large carrot, cut into thick slices
2 garlic cloves, finely grated
2 tablespoons tomato paste
125 ml (½ cup) red wine
2 x 400 g cans crushed tomatoes
1 cinnamon stick
2 whole cloves
2 teaspoons thyme leaves
1 teaspoon caster sugar
cooked basmati rice (see page 21) or
    gluten-free pasta, to serve
chopped parsley leaves, to serve

Season the beef with salt and pepper. Heat 2 tablespoons of the olive oil in a large heavy-based saucepan over medium–high heat. Add the beef in batches and sear for about 5 minutes, turning to brown all over. Remove from the pan and set aside.

Reduce the heat to medium and add the remaining oil. Sauté the onion, celery, carrot and a generous pinch of salt for 5 minutes or until softened. Add the garlic and tomato paste and cook for another 30 seconds.

Pour in the wine and simmer until reduced by half, stirring to release any caramelised bits caught on the base of the pan. Return the beef and any juices to the pan and stir in the crushed tomatoes, cinnamon, cloves, thyme, sugar and 500 ml (2 cups) of water. Season with salt and pepper. Reduce the heat to low, then cover and simmer gently for 2½–3 hours until the beef is tender. If the sauce is still watery after 2 hours, take the lid off and simmer for the last 30 minutes to thicken. Serve with cooked rice or pasta and a sprinkling of parsley over the top.

TIP

- If you own a pressure cooker you can significantly reduce the cooking time by simmering on a low setting for just 40 minutes.

Chinese Five Spice
BEEF SHORT RIBS

SERVES 4–6   DF, GF, LC

Chinese five spice is a great way to quickly inject complex flavour into your food because it contains all five flavour profiles: sweet, sour, bitter, salty and umami. It's usually made up of star anise, cloves, cinnamon, pepper and fennel seeds but it can also contain a variety of other spices. The stunning Asian marinade on these ribs is deliciously addictive and the low and slow cooking method melts the connective tissue in the ribs, resulting in juicy, succulent, fall-apart beef.

2 kg beef short ribs
1 tablespoon Chinese five spice
80 ml (⅓ cup) gluten-free hoisin sauce
80 ml (⅓ cup) gluten-free tamari or
    coconut aminos
2 tablespoons brown sugar
3 garlic cloves, finely grated
1 tablespoon finely grated ginger
250 ml (1 cup) dry sherry

Place the ribs in a roasting tin. Whisk together the Chinese five spice, hoisin, tamari or coconut aminos, sugar, garlic and ginger and rub all over the ribs. Cover and marinate in the fridge for 1 hour or overnight.

Preheat the oven to 160°C (fan-forced).

Pour the sherry into the roasting tin, then cover very tightly with a sheet of baking paper, then foil. Bake for 2½–3 hours until the ribs are fall-apart tender.

Remove the paper and foil and increase the temperature to 200°C (fan-forced). Baste the ribs with the pan juices, then bake for a further 10–15 minutes to caramelise the meat and thicken the sauce. Cut the ribs into bite-size pieces to serve.

Fluffy Beef Keftedes

SERVES 3–4   DF, GF

Keftedes are Greek meatballs infused with fresh parsley and mint and dried oregano. Traditionally, they are made with breadcrumbs soaked in milk but my gluten-free version replaces the breadcrumbs with finely grated potato to achieve a crisp exterior with a light and fluffy centre. Keftedes are super easy to make and extremely versatile. I love them smeared with creamy tzatziki (see page 196) but they also make great sandwich fillings and are fantastic for school lunchboxes.

500 g beef mince
1 large sebago potato (or another floury variety), peeled and finely grated, excess moisture squeezed out
1 onion, grated, excess moisture squeezed out
1 garlic clove, finely grated
1 egg
small handful of flat-leaf parsley leaves, finely chopped, plus extra to serve
small handful of mint leaves, finely chopped
1 teaspoon dried oregano
generous pinch of sea salt flakes and freshly ground black pepper
extra-virgin olive oil, for pan-frying
Tzatziki (see page 196) and lemon wedges, to serve

Place all the ingredients except the olive oil, tzatziki and lemon wedges in a bowl and firmly mix with your hands to combine. Refrigerate for 30 minutes, then roll the mixture into 12 balls.

Heat a good splash of olive oil in a large frying pan over medium heat, add the meatballs (in batches if necessary) and cook for 5–7 minutes, turning until browned all over and cooked through. Remove and drain on paper towel for a few minutes, then sprinkle over a little more chopped parsley and serve with tzatziki and lemon wedges.

Yiayia Sofia's Dolmades
(STUFFED VINE LEAVES)

SERVES 8–10 GF

My mother Sofia is a fantastic cook, and I may be a little biased but I think her dolmades are the tastiest I've ever eaten. She crams them with vibrant herbs for maximum flavour and her mince stuffing is juicy and moist but never mushy. Dolmades can be served as an entree or main meal and they are delicious smeared with a dollop of yoghurt or tzatziki (see page 196). I love mince in my dolmades but you can easily make them vegetarian by omitting the meat, doubling the rice and adding a handful of toasted pine nuts for extra crunch and flavour.

45 fresh vine leaves (see Notes)
125 ml (½ cup) extra-virgin olive oil
1 small red onion, grated, excess moisture squeezed out
2 spring onions, finely sliced
1 tablespoon sea salt flakes
¼ teaspoon ground cumin
250 g beef mince
250 g pork mince
1 vine-ripened tomato, grated, skin discarded
pinch of freshly ground black pepper
100 g (½ cup) medium-grain rice, rinsed
handful of mint leaves, finely chopped
handful of flat-leaf parsley leaves, finely chopped
2 tablespoons finely chopped dill fronds
lemon wedges and Greek yoghurt, to serve

Working in batches, blanch the vine leaves in a saucepan of salted boiling water for 30 seconds. Remove and drain in a large colander.

Heat 3 tablespoons of the olive oil in a large frying pan over low heat, add the red onion, spring onion, salt and cumin and cook for about 5 minutes until softened. Add the beef and pork mince, tomato and pepper and cook for 3 minutes, breaking up the mince with a wooden spoon. Add the rice and fresh herbs and cook for another minute.

Sort through the vine leaves and set aside any that are a bit torn or damaged. Place the remaining leaves on a board, vein-side up. Place 1 tablespoon of the filling on the base of each leaf, then roll up, folding in the sides, to form logs about 5 cm long.

Cover the bottom of a large, wide saucepan with any torn leaves to prevent the dolmades from burning and sticking to the base. Place the dolmades in the pan, seam-side down, sitting next to each other. Continue with a second layer. Drizzle the remaining oil over the dolmades and pour 560 ml (2¼ cups) of water into the side of the pan. Place a dinner plate face down on the dolmades so they don't open during cooking.

Cover and gently simmer over low heat for 40 minutes or until all the water has been absorbed. Remove from the heat and rest for 10 minutes.

Serve the dolmades with lemon wedges and a dollop of Greek yoghurt.

NOTES
- Fresh vine leaves are superior in taste and texture to packaged ones. If you are using the packaged variety there's no need to blanch them – just rinse them thoroughly and drain prior to use.

- You may need more vine leves, depending on their size.

Shepherd's Sweet Potato Pies

SERVES 5 DF, GF

Shepherd's pie is one of those classic family meals that creates smiles around the dinner table. Traditionally, the pie is topped with a white potato mash heavy in cream and butter, but in my dairy-free version I use a sweet potato olive oil mash instead. The natural sweetness from sweet potato pairs beautifully with the rich bolognese sauce, and sweet potato is also very high in antioxidants, vitamins and minerals. My kids love to eat shepherd's pie from individual dishes but this recipe also works in one large baking dish.

2 tablespoons extra-virgin olive oil
1 large onion, finely diced
1 celery stalk, finely diced
1 large carrot, finely diced
2 teaspoons sea salt flakes
3 garlic cloves, finely grated
2 tablespoons tomato paste
700 g beef mince
2 teaspoons thyme leaves
pinch of freshly ground black pepper
500 ml (2 cups) gluten-free beef stock
2 tablespoons finely chopped flat-leaf parsley
  leaves, plus extra to serve

SWEET POTATO MASH

700 g sweet potato, peeled and cut into
  3 cm cubes
2 tablespoons extra-virgin olive oil
2 teaspoons sea salt flakes
pinch of grated nutmeg

Heat the olive oil in a large frying pan over low heat, add the onion, celery, carrot and salt and sauté for 5 minutes or until softened. Add the garlic and tomato paste and cook for another 30 seconds.

Add the mince, thyme and pepper and cook for 5 minutes, breaking up the mince with a wooden spoon. Pour in the stock and simmer for 25 minutes to thicken the sauce. Stir in the parsley.

Preheat the oven to 200°C (fan-forced).

While the sauce is simmering, make the sweet potato mash. Cook the potato in a saucepan of salted boiling water for 15 minutes or until tender. Drain well, then transfer to a food processor, add the remaining ingredients and blitz to a smooth mash.

Divide the bolognese sauce evenly among five 300 ml ramekins. Top with the mash and bake for 30 minutes or until the mash is golden. Sprinkle with extra parsley and serve.

TIP
• The beef can be swapped for lamb mince if preferred – they are equally delicious!

Black Pepper Steak
STIR-FRY

SERVES 4   DF, GF

This is my go-to stir-fry when I want to toss together something yummy in under 20 minutes. Freshly ground pepper adds incredible flavour but it's not too spicy, making it perfect for kids. I find I get the best char on my steak when I let it sear untouched for a minute before flipping over. This maximises contact with the smoking-hot wok for stunning caramelisation. And remember, cook the beef in batches so the meat doesn't stew in an overcrowded wok.

500 g rump steak, finely sliced against the grain
2 tablespoons peanut oil
1 large onion, finely sliced
280 g green beans, trimmed
juice of ½ lemon
1 teaspoon freshly ground black pepper
1 tablespoon gluten-free tamari or coconut aminos
spring onion, finely sliced, to serve
cooked jasmine rice (see page 21), to serve

MARINADE
2 tablespoons gluten-free tamari or coconut aminos
2 garlic cloves, finely grated
2 teaspoons brown sugar
1 teaspoon sesame oil

To make the marinade, combine all the ingredients in a glass or ceramic dish. Add the beef and turn to coat, then marinate for 15 minutes at room temperature or in the fridge overnight (bring the beef back to room temperature prior to cooking).

Heat a wok over high heat until smoking hot. Add 1 tablespoon of the peanut oil, then add the beef in batches and let it cook until nicely charred and caramelised. Remove the beef and set aside.

Add the remaining oil to the wok and stir-fry the onion and beans for 2 minutes. Add the lemon juice and toss to combine. Return the beef and any resting juices to the wok, add the pepper and tamari or coconut aminos and stir-fry for another minute to combine. Sprinkle with spring onion and serve with jasmine rice.

Slow-cooked Beef Cheeks
WITH POLENTA

SERVES 4–6   DF, GF

This is a stunning recipe that requires very little effort; it only needs time. Beef cheeks are full of collagen, which needs slow cooking to break down, leaving you with a melt-in-the-mouth dish worthy of any fine-dining restaurant. I've kept the polenta dairy free by preparing it with olive oil instead of butter – it's just as creamy and delicious. You could also swap the polenta for whipped potato mash.

1.2 kg beef cheeks (roughly 4–6 cheeks)
sea salt flakes and freshly ground black pepper
2 tablespoons extra-virgin olive oil
1 large onion, diced
1 large carrot, diced
3 garlic cloves, sliced
2 tablespoons tomato paste
500 ml (2 cups) red wine
3 tablespoons sherry vinegar
3 dried bay leaves
1 cinnamon stick
polenta (page 21), to serve
chopped flat-leaf parsley leaves, to serve

Preheat the oven to 180°C (fan-forced).

Season the beef cheeks with salt and pepper. Heat the olive oil in a large flameproof casserole dish over medium–high heat. Add the beef in batches and sear for 5 minutes, turning to brown all over. Remove from the dish and set aside.

Reduce the heat to medium, add the onion, carrot and a generous pinch of salt and sauté for 5 minutes. Add the garlic and tomato paste and cook, stirring, for another 30 seconds. Return the beef to the dish, then pour in the wine, vinegar and 500 ml (2 cups) of water and add the bay leaves and cinnamon stick. Cover and braise in the oven for 3 hours, adding extra water if required.

Remove the beef cheeks and set aside. Strain the cooking liquid into a small saucepan, discarding the solids, and simmer over low heat until reduced to a gravy. Return the beef cheeks and gravy to the casserole dish and stir to coat and combine.

To serve, spoon the polenta into shallow bowls, top with the beef cheeks and gravy and finish with parsley.

SWEET

Olive Oil Vanilla Cupcakes
WITH STRAWBERRY ICING

MAKES 12   DF, GF, V

These light and fluffy cupcakes are perfect for kids' birthday parties because they are dairy, gluten and nut free so no one has to miss out. They're super quick to whip together, and all you need is a bowl and spoon. Freeze-dried strawberry powder is far superior in flavour to fake strawberry essence (steer clear of essences please!) and it will tint your icing the prettiest pale pink colour. Even the adults will be fighting over the last cupcake!

260 g (2 cups) plain gluten-free flour
1 tablespoon gluten-free baking powder
170 g (¾ cup) caster sugar
170 ml (⅔ cup) light olive oil
185 ml (¾ cup) coconut milk or preferred milk
2 eggs, lightly whisked
1 tablespoon vanilla extract
gluten-free sprinkles, for decorating

STRAWBERRY ICING
210 g pure icing sugar, sifted
1 tablespoon freeze-dried strawberry powder
1 egg white
60 ml (¼ cup) lemon juice

Preheat the oven to 180°C (fan-forced). Grease or line a 12-cup muffin tin with paper cases.

Combine the flour, baking powder and caster sugar in a bowl and make a well in the centre. Add the olive oil, milk, egg and vanilla extract and whisk to combine.

Spoon the batter into the paper cases and bake for 20–25 minutes or until a skewer inserted in the centre of a muffin comes out clean. Remove from the tray and cool completely on a wire rack.

To make the strawberry icing, whisk the ingredients in a bowl until combined. Spoon the icing over the cupcakes and decorate with sprinkles before it sets. The cakes will keep in an airtight container at room temperature for up to 3 days.

TIP
- If you can't find any freeze-dried strawberry powder, make a strawberry puree instead. Simmer 3–4 chopped strawberries with a little water for a couple of minutes and mash it into a puree.

Pasteli
(TOASTED SESAME BARS)

MAKES 30   DF, GF, V

If you love a bit of crunch, these bars are for you. They are very simple to prepare with few ingredients, but mastering the perfect crunch can be elusive. The trick is to simmer the honey mixture long enough to strengthen the bond of the honey glue – too short a simmer and your bars will be soft, not crunchy (though still delicious). The peanuts can be swapped for almonds, macadamias, pistachios or cashews, or you can omit the nuts altogether and double the sesame quantity for a nut-free version.

500 g unsalted peanuts
500 g sesame seeds
175 g (½ cup) honey
115 g (½ cup) caster sugar
pinch of sea salt flakes

Preheat the oven to 200°C (fan-forced) and line a large baking sheet with baking paper.

Spread out the peanuts and sesame seeds on a large baking tray and toast in the oven for 15 minutes or until lightly golden, tossing occasionally to ensure even browning. Remove and set aside.

Place the honey, sugar and salt in a large saucepan and stir over low heat until melted and combined. Simmer gently for 5 minutes, stirring occasionally, until the mixture turns golden – it will become foamy as it simmers.

Add the peanuts and sesame seeds and stir to combine. Tip the mixture onto the prepared sheet, using a spatula to scrape the nuts and seeds out of the pan. Immediately place another sheet of baking paper on top and roll out to a rectangular slab roughly 40 cm × 25 cm and 1 cm thick.

Peel away the top layer of baking paper and, while the pasteli is still warm, cut the slab into bars (the slab will completely harden when it cools so you must slice it before it does). Leave the bars to cool and set, then store in an airtight container at room temperature for 2–3 weeks.

I Can't Believe There's No Butter
CHOC CHIP COOKIES

MAKES 18   DF, GF, V

Crispy edges + chewy centre + molten chocolate chunks = cookie heaven. Coconut oil is my go to when baking dairy-free cookies because it delivers that perfect utopia of crispness and chewiness. Adjusting the baking time by a few minutes either way will make your cookies softer or crunchier so do customise it to suit your preference. One bite and you'll never reach for that butter again!

130 g coconut oil, at room temperature
½ cup (115 g) brown sugar
½ cup (115 g) caster sugar
2 teaspoons vanilla extract
1 egg
230 g (1¾ cups) plain gluten-free flour
1 teaspoon gluten-free baking powder
½ teaspoon bicarbonate of soda
1 teaspoon sea salt flakes
200 g gluten-free dark chocolate
    (70% cocoa), chopped into 1–2 cm chunks

Place the coconut oil and both sugars in the bowl of an electric mixer fitted with the paddle attachment and beat for 1 minute. Add the vanilla and egg and beat to combine.

Add the flour, baking powder, bicarbonate of soda and salt and beat until just combined, then fold in the chopped chocolate. Place the dough in the fridge for 30 minutes (or overnight for crispier cookies).

Preheat the oven to 180°C (fan-forced) and line two baking trays with baking paper.

Roll the dough into 18 balls, place on the prepared trays evenly spaced apart and gently flatten with the palm of your hand (see Tip). Bake for 15 minutes or until golden and crisp. Transfer to a wire rack to cool. Store the cookies in an airtight container at room temperature for up to 2 weeks.

TIP
- The size and shape of the dough dictates the spread of the cookie so if you want your cookies thin and crispy, flatten the balls with the palm of your hand. For a more rounded shape and softer texture leave them as balls.

Molten Chocolate Puddings

SERVES 4   DF, GF, V

Warm, oozy, intensely dark and chocolatey … no wonder this is my favourite dessert of all time. These puddings are always greeted with 'oohs' and 'aahs' when spooned open to reveal the chocolate lava inside. The key ingredient here is coconut oil, which, on top of being dairy and gluten free, keeps the cakes incredibly moist. They are so quick and simple to prepare but guaranteed to satisfy your chocolate craving in the most dramatic and theatrical fashion.

225 g coconut oil, plus extra for greasing
300 g gluten-free dark chocolate
   (70% cocoa), chopped
170 g (¾ cup) caster sugar
4 eggs
2 teaspoons vanilla extract
3 tablespoons plain gluten-free flour
pinch of sea salt flakes
dutch-process cocoa powder and raspberries,
   to serve
dairy-free ice cream (optional), to serve

Preheat the oven to 160°C (fan-forced) and grease four 300 ml ramekins with coconut oil.

Place the coconut oil and chocolate in a small saucepan and melt over low heat, stirring until smooth and combined. Set aside.

Place the sugar, eggs and vanilla in the bowl of an electric mixer fitted with the paddle attachment and beat for 3 minutes or until pale and creamy. With the mixer running on low speed, pour the chocolate mixture down the side of the bowl and mix until just combined. Sift the flour over the batter, add the salt and gently fold through.

Divide the batter evenly among the ramekins, then place on a baking tray and bake for 15–18 minutes until the puddings are firm to the touch on top but still oozy in the centre (test with a skewer if you like). Cooking time is critical to perfect the chocolate ooze, so check the puddings after 15 minutes to see if they are ready before cooking further.

Place a plate over each ramekin and carefully flip the puddings onto them. Gently lift off the ramekins to reveal the puddings. Dust with cocoa powder and serve warm with raspberries and a scoop of your favourite ice cream, if using.

Coconut Tiramisu

SERVES 8–10   DF, GF, V

This recipe was a massive hit on my cooking show *Loving Gluten Free*. Many viewers had not eaten a tiramisu in years and almost nobody had tasted a dairy-free version. Chilled coconut cream whips up beautifully and is a great replacement for mascarpone. And don't worry if you're not a huge fan of coconut – the flavours from the espresso and liqueur overpower it so it just tastes like regular cream with the slightest hint of coconut. I like my tiramisu light and spongey but if you prefer it on the creamy side just add another can of coconut cream.

3–4 × 270 ml cans coconut cream, chilled overnight
1 vanilla bean, split and seeds scraped
60 g (½ cup) pure icing sugar, sifted
750 ml (3 cups) freshly brewed coffee, lukewarm
80 ml (⅓ cup) Kahlua or Tia Maria liqueur
200 g packet gluten-free savoiardi biscuits (see Tips)
dutch-process cocoa powder, for dusting

Scoop out the hardened coconut cream from the lids of the cans and transfer to the bowl of an electric mixer fitted with the whisk attachment. To separate the rest of the hardened cream from the coconut water, tip the remaining contents into a sieve set over a bowl so the coconut water drains from the cream. (This should leave you with roughly 550 g of cream; reserve the coconut water and use it in smoothies or curries.) Add the cream to the bowl of the mixer, along with the vanilla seeds and icing sugar, and whip for 1–2 minutes until soft peaks form.

Combine the coffee and liqueur in a shallow dish. Gently dip the biscuits into the coffee mixture and arrange half of them in a single layer in a serving dish roughly 25 cm × 20 cm. Spread half of the whipped coconut cream over the biscuit layer. Repeat with the remaining soaked biscuits and cream, then cover with plastic wrap and refrigerate for at least 4 hours or overnight to set.

Remove the plastic wrap, dust generously with sifted cocoa powder and serve.

TIPS

- You can purchase gluten-free savoiardi biscuits at gourmet grocers or online.

- If you prefer not to include alcohol simply omit and dissolve 1 tablespoon of cocoa powder in the coffee for a mocha tiramisu.

Rizogalo
(GREEK RICE PUDDING)

SERVES 4   GF, V

Rizogalo is a creamy Greek rice pudding whose name is derived from two words: rizi (rice) and gala (milk). Some home cooks thicken their rizogalo with cornflour but this is unnecessary if you use the correct rice, namely arborio. Due to its high starch content, arborio naturally thickens the milk when simmered and it also holds its shape well – one of my pet hates is mushy rice in rizogalo! I don't make my rizogalo overly sweet but feel free to increase the quantity of sugar to suit your palate.

125 g arborio rice
250 ml (1 cup) full-cream milk
180 ml (¾ cup) pouring cream
80 g (⅓ cup) caster sugar
1 vanilla bean, split and seeds scraped
1 cinnamon stick
ground cinnamon, to serve

Place all the ingredients except the ground cinnamon in a saucepan. Add 250 ml (1 cup) of water and bring to a simmer over high heat, stirring to combine. Reduce the heat to low and gently simmer, stirring occasionally, for 20 minutes or until the rice is tender.

Pour the rizogalo into bowls and sprinkle with ground cinnamon while still warm – the pudding will thicken as it cools. Rest for 5 minutes and eat warm or refrigerate and enjoy cold.

VARIATIONS

- I love a traditional rizogalo prepared with vanilla and cinnamon but you can add other aromatics, such as orange zest, lemon zest and cardamom, when simmering the rice, and garnish with chopped nuts and dried fruit.

- For a dairy-free rizogalo replace the milk and cream with coconut milk and coconut cream.

Simple Chocolate
& HAZELNUT CAKE

SERVES 12   DF, GF, V

When I was growing up I loved smearing chocolate hazelnut spread on white bread as an afternoon treat. Thankfully supermarkets now stock organic dairy-free chocolate hazelnut spreads that are much tastier and cleaner than the leading brands. Hazelnut meal is fantastic for baking because it has a buttery, nutty flavour and keeps cakes incredibly moist without the need for added fat. This cake is super quick to whip up and the two-ingredient chocolate ganache couldn't be easier.

6 eggs
310 g (1⅓ cups) caster sugar
330 g (3 cups) hazelnut meal (see Note)
2 teaspoons gluten-free baking powder
pinch of sea salt flakes
chopped hazelnuts, to decorate

GANACHE
150 g (¾ cup) dairy-free chocolate
   hazelnut spread
60 ml (¼ cup) coconut cream

Preheat the oven to 160°C (fan-forced). Grease and line a 20 cm round cake tin with baking paper.

Using an electric mixer, beat the eggs and sugar for 3 minutes or until light and fluffy. Add the hazelnut meal, baking powder and salt and mix until just combined.

Pour the batter into the prepared tin and bake for 50 minutes or until a skewer inserted in the centre comes out clean. Cool in the tin for 10 minutes, then turn out onto a wire rack to cool completely.

To make the ganache, place the chocolate hazelnut spread and coconut cream in a small saucepan over low heat and stir until smooth and well combined.

Pour the ganache over the cooled cake. Using a spatula, spread it right to the edge and smooth the surface, allowing a little ganache to drizzle down the side of the cake. Decorate with chopped hazelnuts, then cut into slices and serve. Leftover cake will keep in an airtight container at room temperature for up to 5 days.

NOTE
- You can replace the hazelnut meal with almond meal if you like. It will have a finer texture and a milder flavour but will be just as delicious.

Raw Mango
& MACADAMIA CHEESECAKE

SERVES 16   DF, GF, VG

Packed with nutrient-dense ingredients, raw vegan desserts have exploded onto the cafe scene in recent years as more and more people seek delicious 'clean' treats. All you need here is a food processor to blitz together your gluten-, dairy- and refined sugar-free ingredients to create three stunning layers. I love this tropical combo of mango, macadamia and coconut with a squeeze of zesty lime juice to make all the flavours sing. Macadamias are waxy so they are fantastic for 'creaming', but cashews work equally well.

grated lime zest and toasted coconut flakes,
   to serve

BASE
90 g (1½ cups) shredded coconut
160 g (1 cup) raw macadamias
8 medjool dates, pitted
½ teaspoon sea salt flakes
½ teaspoon ground cinnamon

FILLING
240 g (1½ cups) raw macadamias,
   soaked in cold water overnight, drained
270 ml can coconut cream
125 ml (½ cup) pure maple syrup
2 tablespoons coconut oil
finely grated zest and juice of 1 lime
2 teaspoons vanilla extract

TOPPING
160 g (1 cup) raw macadamias, soaked in cold
   water overnight, drained
125 ml (½ cup) coconut cream
2 ripe mangoes, chopped
80 ml (⅓ cup) pure maple syrup
1 tablespoon coconut oil
finely grated zest and juice of 1 lime
pinch of sea salt flakes

Line a 20 cm square cake tin with a removable base with baking paper.

To make the base, place all the ingredients in a food processor and blitz for 30 seconds to form a textured paste. Tip the paste into the tin and press firmly and evenly into the base. Rest in the freezer.

For the filling, blitz the macadamias in a food processor to form a paste. Add the remaining ingredients and blitz until smooth. Pour the filling into the tin, then return to the freezer for 2 hours to firm up.

To make the topping, blitz the macadamias in a food processor to form a paste. Add the remaining ingredients and blitz until smooth. Pour over the filling and smooth out with a spatula. Freeze for 4 hours.

Thaw the cake for 10 minutes, then use a hot knife to cut into 6 square pieces.

This cheesecake is best eaten semi-frozen. Before serving, top with grated lime zest and toasted coconut flakes. Store your raw cake in an airtight container in the freezer for up to 2 weeks.

30-second Banana
NICE-CREAM BOWLS

SERVES 4   DF, GF, VG

So what exactly is 'nice-cream'? It's basically a super-soft ice cream made by pureeing frozen bananas. This vegan dessert takes seconds to whiz up and is a much healthier option than ice cream because most of the sweetness comes from ripe banana, not processed sugar. My freezer is always stocked with chopped bananas so I can satisfy my craving in just 30 seconds – the hardest part is narrowing down the toppings!

400 g frozen ripe bananas, chopped
3 tablespoons coconut cream
1 tablespoon pure maple syrup
¼ teaspoon ground cinnamon
your choice of chopped nuts, fruit, seeds, coconut and/or cacao nibs, to serve

Blitz the bananas in a food processor until smooth. Add the coconut cream, maple syrup and cinnamon and process to combine. Serve with your favourite toppings for textural crunch and flavour.

CONVERSION CHARTS

Measuring cups and spoons may vary slightly from one country to another, but the difference is generally not enough to affect a recipe. All cup and spoon measures are level.

One Australian metric measuring cup holds 250 ml (8 fl oz), one Australian metric tablespoon holds 20 ml (4 teaspoons) and one Australian metric teaspoon holds 5 ml. North America, New Zealand and the UK use a 15 ml (3-teaspoon) tablespoon.

LENGTH

METRIC	IMPERIAL
3 mm	⅛ inch
6 mm	¼ inch
1 cm	½ inch
2.5 cm	1 inch
5 cm	2 inches
18 cm	7 inches
20 cm	8 inches
23 cm	9 inches
25 cm	10 inches
30 cm	12 inches

LIQUID MEASURES

ONE AMERICAN PINT	ONE IMPERIAL PINT
500 ml (16 fl oz)	600 ml (20 fl oz)

CUP	METRIC	IMPERIAL
⅛ cup	30 ml	1 fl oz
¼ cup	60 ml	2 fl oz
⅓ cup	80 ml	2½ fl oz
½ cup	125 ml	4 fl oz
⅔ cup	160 ml	5 fl oz
¾ cup	180 ml	6 fl oz
1 cup	250 ml	8 fl oz
2 cups	500 ml	16 fl oz
2¼ cups	560 ml	20 fl oz
4 cups	1 litre	32 fl oz

DRY MEASURES

The most accurate way to measure dry ingredients is to weigh them. However, if using a cup, add the ingredient loosely to the cup and level with a knife; don't compact the ingredient unless the recipe requests 'firmly packed'.

METRIC	IMPERIAL
15 g	½ oz
30 g	1 oz
60 g	2 oz
125 g	4 oz (¼ lb)
185 g	6 oz
250 g	8 oz (½ lb)
375 g	12 oz (¾ lb)
500 g	16 oz (1 lb)
1 kg	32 oz (2 lb)

OVEN TEMPERATURES

CELSIUS	FAHRENHEIT
100°C	200°F
120°C	250°F
150°C	300°F
160°C	325°F
180°C	350°F
200°C	400°F
220°C	425°F

CELSIUS	GAS MARK
110°C	¼
130°C	½
140°C	1
150°C	2
170°C	3
180°C	4
190°C	5
200°C	6
220°C	7
230°C	8
240°C	9
250°C	10

THANKS

Mary, Clare and Ashley. When I first met you at the Plum Melbourne office you were so warm and welcoming. I instantly knew I had found my tribe. I recall immediately hitting it off and excitedly yapping away about the book, recipe ideas, motherhood, reality TV and so much more that I almost missed my return flight home to Sydney. Thank you for welcoming me with open arms and for making the whole process seamless and so enjoyable.

Jeremy and Vanessa, the incredibly talented dynamic duo. From the first day on set I could see why you work together so frequently. You really create magic and you are two of the nicest creatives I have ever met. Thank you for bringing my recipes to life and for helping me tell a beautiful story with every image. You took such great care in capturing those gorgeous rays of natural light and perfecting little things like the right amount of chocolate ooze in that molten pudding. I loved watching you work and have a newfound respect for the use of tweezers and for herbs swimming in cold ice baths!

Sarah and Melissa, thank you for being kitchen wizards. You perfected every dish and kept a jam-packed shooting schedule on track. Thank you for testing my recipes with great diligence and ensuring I wasn't being too stingy with the number of prawns I specified in my salad.

Rachel, thank you for doing such a great job editing. You have an amazing eye for detail, the yin to my yang. I'm so glad spanakorizo became your new mid-week family favourite whilst editing and that I could nourish you along the way.

Emily, thank you for the stunning design. You have wonderfully captured my personality and love of all things pastel and pink. I feel like the book is an extension of my family home, so thank you for creating a look and feel that fits me perfectly.

To Tracey Cheetham and the entire publicity team, thanks for working tirelessly to spread the book's gluten-free message as far and wide as possible. To everyone else behind the scenes at Pan Macmillan, thank you so much for all your incredible efforts. It takes a huge team to put this book into everyone's hands so thank you.

To the team at H Squared and SBS Food, thank you for giving me the opportunity to host Australia's first gluten-free cooking show, *Loving Gluten Free*. Never in a million years did I think my little gluten-free blog would lead to a television show and two cookbooks.

Thank you to the team at Coeliac Australia for your continued support and for allowing me to partner with you and raise awareness of gluten intolerances in our community.

To my husband, Spiro, and my three angels, Vasili, Sofia and Ruby, I could not have begun or continued along this journey without your love and support. Thank you for filling these pages with your beautiful smiles and hearts. Thank you to my extended family, Katerina, Jack, Dylan, Ellis, Gerry, Teresa, Eliana, Billy and grandparents George, Sofia, Bill and Maria. You have been my number-one cheerleaders (and publicists!) so thank you for that. To my friends and many cousins, thanks for always celebrating my successes and 'checking in' with a simple phone call or text encouraging me along the way.

Finally, thank you to everyone who has purchased my books, watched my television series, attended one of my cooking demos, followed me on social media or stopped me in the supermarket to let me know you loved my carrot cake recipe. None of this would be possible without your support so thank you from the bottom of my heart for allowing me to share my love of gluten-free cooking with the world.

Lots of love,

Helen

INDEX

A PLUM BOOK

First published in 2020 by
Pan Macmillan Australia Pty Limited
Level 25, 1 Market Street, Sydney,
NSW 2000, Australia
Level 3, 112 Wellington Parade,
East Melbourne, VIC 3002, Australia

Text copyright © Helen Tzouganatos 2020

Photographs Jeremy Simons copyright
© Pan Macmillan 2020

Design Emily O'Neill copyright
© Pan Macmillan 2020

The moral right of the author
has been asserted.

Design by Emily O'Neill
Edited by Rachel Carter
Index by Helena Holmgren
Photography by Jeremy Simons
Prop and food styling by Vanessa Austin
Food preparation by Sarah Mayoh and Melissa Hurwitz
Typeset by Emily O'Neill
Colour reproduction by Splitting Image Colour Studio
Printed and bound in China by Hang Tai Printing Co. Ltd.

A CIP catalogue record for this book is available from the
National Library of Australia.

10 9 8 7 6 5 4 3 2 1